4/14

German Phrases
FOR
DUMMIES®

by Paulina Christens_
and Anne Fo_

Wiley Publishing,

German Phrases For Dummies®

Published by
Wiley Publishing, Inc.
111 River St.
Hoboken, NJ 07030-5774
www.wiley.com

Copyright © 2005 by Wiley Publishing, Inc., Indianapolis, Indiana

Published by Wiley Publishing, Inc., Indianapolis, Indiana

Published simultaneously in Canada

For general information on our other products and services, please contact our Customer Care Department within the U.S. at 800-762-2974, outside the U.S. at 317-572-3993, or fax 317-572-4002.

For technical support, please visit www.wiley.com/techsupport.

Wiley also publishes its books in a variety of electronic formats. Some content that appears in print may not be available in electronic books.

Library of Congress Control Number: 2005924608

ISBN-13: 978-07645-9553-0

ISBN-10: 0-7645-9553-9

Manufactured in the United States of America

10 9 8 7 6 5 4 3

1O/QR/QY/QV/IN

About the Authors

Paulina Christensen has been working as a writer, editor, and translator for almost ten years. She holds a degree in English and German literature and has developed, written, and edited numerous German-language textbooks and teachers' handbooks for Berlitz International. Her work as a translator ranges from new media art to science fiction (*Starlog* magazine). She occasionally works as a court interpreter and does consulting and interpreting at educational conferences, as well as voice-overs for educational videos and CD-ROMs. Dr. Christensen received her M.A. and Ph.D. from Düsseldorf University, Germany, and has taught at Berlitz Language Schools, New York University, and Fordham University.

Anne Fox has been working as a translator, editor, and writer for the past twelve years. She studied at Interpreters' School, Zurich, Switzerland, and holds a degree in translation. Her various assignments have taken her to outer space, hyperspace, and around the world. She has also taught at Berlitz Language Schools and worked as a legal and technical proofreader in the editorial departments of several law firms. Most recently she has been developing, writing, and editing student textbooks and teacher handbooks for Berlitz.

Publisher's Acknowledgments

We're proud of this book; please send us your comments through our Dummies online registration form located at www.dummies.com/register/.

Some of the people who helped bring this book to market include the following:

Acquisitions, Editorial, and Media Development

Compiler:
Laura Peterson-Nussbaum

Senior Project Editor:
Tim Gallan

Acquisitions Editor:
Stacy Kennedy

Copy Editor: Chad R. Sievers

Technical Editor: Language Training Center

Editorial Manager:
Christine Meloy Beck

Editorial Assistants:
Courtney Allen,
Nadine Bell

Cartoons: Rich Tennant,
www.the5thwave.com

Composition

Project Coordinator:
Adrienne Martinez

Layout and Graphics:
Stephanie D. Jumper,
Lauren Goddard

Proofreaders:
Mildred Rosenzweig,
Joe Niesen,
Charles Spencer

Indexer: Joan Griffitts

Publishing and Editorial for Consumer Dummies

Diane Graves Steele, Vice President and Publisher, Consumer Dummies

Joyce Pepple, Acquisitions Director, Consumer Dummies

Kristin A. Cocks, Product Development Director, Consumer Dummies

Michael Spring, Vice President and Publisher, Travel

Brice Gosnell, Associate Publisher, Travel

Kelly Regan, Editorial Director, Travel

Publishing for Technology Dummies

Andy Cummings, Vice President and Publisher, Dummies Technology/General User

Composition Services

Gerry Fahey, Vice President of Production Services

Debbie Stailey, Director of Composition Services

Table of Contents

The 5th Wave

By Rich Tennant

@RICHTENNANT

"I'd ask for directions in German, but I don't know how to form a question into the shape of an apology."

Introduction

$\bullet$ $\bullet$

*A*s society becomes more and more international in nature, knowing how to say at least a few words in other languages becomes more and more useful. Inexpensive airfares make travel abroad a more realistic option. Global business environments necessitate overseas travel. You may even have a few friends and neighbors who speak other languages. Or you may want to get in touch with your heritage by studying a little bit of the language that your ancestors spoke.

Whatever your reason for wanting to master some German, this book can help. We're not promising fluency, but if you need to greet someone, purchase a ticket, or order off a menu in German, you need look no further than *German Phrases For Dummies*.

About This Book

This book isn't a class that you have to drag yourself to twice a week for a specified period of time. You can use *German Phrases For Dummies* however you want to, whether your goal is to master some words and phrases to help you get around when you visit Germany (or any other German-speaking country), or you just want to be able to say "Hello, how are you?" to your German-speaking neighbor. Go through this book at your own pace, reading as much or as little at a time as you like. You don't have to trudge through the chapters in order, either; just read the sections that interest you.

Note: If you've never taken German before, you may want to read Chapters 1 and 2 before you tackle the later chapters. They give you some of the basics that you need to know about the language, such as how to pronounce the various sounds.

Conventions Used in This Book

To make this book easy for you to navigate, we've set up a couple of conventions:

- ✔ German terms are set in **boldface** to make them stand out.

- ✔ Pronunciations set in *italics* follow the German terms.

- ✔ Stressed syllables are <u>underlined</u> in the pronunciation.

- ✔ Memorizing key words and phrases is important in language learning, so we collect the important words in a chapter or section in a chalkboard with the heading "Words to Know." German nouns have genders, which determine which article it takes. In the Words to Know blackboards, we include the article for each noun so that you can memorize it at the same time as the noun.

- ✔ Verb conjugations (lists that show you the forms of a verb) are given in tables in this order: the "I" form, the "you" (singular, informal) form, the "you" (singular, formal) form, the "he/she/it" form, the "we" form, the "you" (plural, informal) form, the "you" (plural, formal) form, and the "they" form. Pronunciations follow in the second column. Here's an example:

Conjugation	*Pronunciation*
ich werde	îH <u>vehr</u>-de
du wirst	dû vîrst
Sie werden	zee <u>vehr</u>-dn
er, sie, es wird	ehr/zee/ês vîrt
wir werden	veer <u>vehr</u>-dn
ihr werdet	eer <u>vehr</u>-det
Sie werden	zee <u>vehr</u>-dn
sie werden	zee <u>vehr</u>-dn

Also note that, because each language has its own ways of expressing ideas, the English translations that we provide for the German terms may not be exactly literal. We want you to know the gist of what's being said, not just the words that are being said. For example, the phrase **Es geht** _(ês geht)_ can be translated literally as "It goes," but the phrase really means "So, so." This book gives the "So, so" translation.

Foolish Assumptions

To write this book, we make some assumptions about who you are and what you want from a book called _German Phrases For Dummies_. Here are the assumptions that we make about you:

- ✔ You know no German — or if you took German back in school, you don't remember a word of it.

- ✔ You're not looking for a book that will make you fluent in German; you just want to know some words, phrases, and sentence constructions so that you can communicate basic information in German.

- ✔ You don't want to have to memorize long lists of vocabulary words or a bunch of boring grammar rules.

- ✔ You want to have fun and learn a little bit of German at the same time.

Icons Used in This Book

You may be looking for particular information while reading this book. To make certain types of information easier for you to find, we've placed the following icons in the left-hand margins throughout the book:

This icon highlights tips that can make learning German easier.

This icon points out interesting information that you don't want to forget.

Languages are full of quirks that may trip you up if you're not prepared for them. This icon points to discussions of these weird grammar rules.

If you're looking for information about German culture or travel, look for these icons. They draw your attention to interesting tidbits about the countries in which German is spoken.

Where to Go from Here

Learning a language is all about jumping in and giving it a try (no matter how bad your pronunciation is at first). So make the leap! Start at the beginning or pick a chapter that interests you. Before long, you'll be able to respond, "Ja!" when people ask, "Sprechen Sie Deutsch?"

Chapter 1

I Say It How?
Speaking German

. . . .

In This Chapter

▶ Recognizing the German you already know

▶ Pronouncing the basics

▶ Using popular expressions

. . . .

*T*he best way to learn a new language is total
immersion — so in this chapter, you jump right
into the German language. This chapter shows you
the German you may already know, explains how to
pronounce German, and introduces you to some popular German expressions.

The German You Know

Because both German and English belong to the
group of Germanic languages, they have quite a few
identical or similar words. These words are called
cognates.

Friendly allies (perfect cognates)

The following words are spelled the same way and
have the same meaning in German and English. The
only differences are the pronunciation and the fact
that in German, nouns are always capitalized:

- ✔ **der Arm** *(dehr ârm)*
- ✔ **der Bandit** *(dehr bân-_deet_)*
- ✔ **die Bank** *(dee bânk)*
- ✔ **die Basis** *(dee _bah_-zîs)*
- ✔ **blind** *(blînt)*
- ✔ **die Butter** *(dee _bû_-ter)*
- ✔ **elegant** *(êle-_gânt_)*
- ✔ **die Emotion** *(dee êmoh-_tsîohn_)*
- ✔ **emotional** *(êmoh-tsîoh-_nahl_)*
- ✔ **der Finger** *(dehr _fîn_-ger)*
- ✔ **die Garage** *(dee gâ-_rah_-je)*
- ✔ **die Hand** *(dee hânt)*
- ✔ **das Hotel** *(dâs hoh-_têl_)*
- ✔ **die Inspiration** *(dee în-spee-râ-_tsîohn_)*
- ✔ **international** *(în-ter-nâtsîo-_nahl_)*
- ✔ **irrational** *(_îrâ_-tsîoh-_nahl_)*
- ✔ **der Kitsch** *(dehr kîtsh)*
- ✔ **modern** *(moh-_dêrn_)*
- ✔ **der Moment** *(dehr moh-_mênt_)*
- ✔ **das Museum** *(dâs mû-_zeh_-ûm)*
- ✔ **der Name** *(dehr _nah_-me)*
- ✔ **die Nation** *(dee nâts-_îohn_)*
- ✔ **die Olive** *(dee oh-_lee_-ve)*
- ✔ **die Orange** *(dee oh-_rong_-je)*
- ✔ **parallel** *(pârâ-_lehl_)*
- ✔ **das Photo** *(dâs _foh_-toh)*
- ✔ **das Problem** *(dâs prô-_blehm_)*
- ✔ **die Religion** *(dee rêlî-_gîohn_)*
- ✔ **das Restaurant** *(dâs rês-toh-_rong_)*
- ✔ **die Rose** *(dee _roh_-ze)*
- ✔ **der Service** *(dehr _ser_-vîs)*

- ✔ **das Signal** *(dâs zîg-nahl)*
- ✔ **der Sport** *(dehr shpôrt)*
- ✔ **die Statue** *(dee shtah-tooe)*
- ✔ **das System** *(dâs zuus-tehm)*
- ✔ **das Taxi** *(dâs tâ-xee)*
- ✔ **der Tiger** *(dehr tee-ger)*
- ✔ **der Tunnel** *(dehr tû-nel)*
- ✔ **wild** *(vîlt)*
- ✔ **der Wind** *(dehr vînt)*

Kissing cousins (near cognates)

Many words, like the ones in Table 1-1, are spelled almost the same in German as in English and have the same meaning.

Notice that the English "c" is a "k" in most German words.

Table 1-1	Words Similar in Meaning, Slightly Different in Spelling
German	**English**
die Adresse *(dee ah-drê-sse)*	address
der Aspekt *(dehr âs-pêkt)*	aspect
blond *(blônt)*	blond/blonde
die Bluse *(dee bloo-ze)*	blouse
die Demokratie *(dee dêmô-krah-tee)*	democracy
direkt *(dî-rêkt)*	direct
der Doktor *(dehr dôk-tohr)*	doctor
exzellent *(êxtse-lênt)*	excellent

(continued)

Table 1-1 *(continued)*

German	English
fantastisch *(fân-<u>tâs</u>-tish)*	fantastic
das Glas *(dâs glahs)*	glass
der Kaffee *(dehr <u>kâ</u>-feh)*	coffee
die Komödie *(dee kô-<u>muo</u>-dee-e)*	comedy
die Kondition *(dee kôn-dî-<u>tsîohn</u>)*	condition
das Konzert *(dâs kôn-<u>tsêrt</u>)*	concert
die Kultur *(dee kûl-<u>toor</u>)*	culture
lang *(lâng)*	long
die Maschine *(dee mâ-<u>shee</u>-ne)*	machine
die Maus *(dee mows)*	mouse
die Methode *(dee mê-<u>toh</u>-de)*	method
die Musik *(dee mû-<u>zeek</u>)*	music
die Nationalität *(dee <u>nât</u>-sîo-nahl-î-<u>tait</u>)*	nationality
die Natur *(dee nâ-<u>toor</u>)*	nature
der Ozean *(dehr <u>oh</u>-tseh-ahn)*	ocean
das Papier *(dâs pâ-<u>peer</u>)*	paper
perfekt *(pêr-<u>fêkt</u>)*	perfect
potenziell *(pô-tên-<u>tsîel</u>)*	potential (adjective)
das Programm *(dâs proh-<u>grâm</u>)*	program
das Salz *(dâs zâlts)*	salt
der Scheck *(dehr shêk)*	check
der Supermarkt *(dehr <u>zoo</u>-pêr-mârkt)*	supermarket
das Telefon *(dâs <u>tê</u>-le-fohn)*	telephone

German	English
die Theorie *(dee teh-oh-<u>ree</u>)*	theory
die Tragödie *(dee trâ-<u>guo</u>-dee-e)*	tragedy
die Walnuss *(dee <u>vahl</u>-nûs)*	walnut

False friends

As in every language, German contains some false friends — those words that look very similar to English words but often have a completely different meaning:

- ✔ **After** *(<u>âf</u>-ter)*: If you want to avoid embarrassment, remember the meaning of this word. It means "anus" and not "after." The German word for "after" is **nach** *(nahH)* or **nachdem** *(nahH-dehm)*.

- ✔ **aktuell** *(âk-too-<u>êl</u>)*: This word means "up-to-date" and "current," not "actually." The German translation for "actually" is **tatsächlich** *(taht-<u>sêH</u>-līH)*.

- ✔ **also** *(<u>âl</u>-zoh)*: This one means "so, therefore" and not "also." The German word for "also" is **auch** *(owH)*.

- ✔ **bekommen** *(be-<u>kô</u>-men)*: This verb is an important one to remember. It means "to get" and not "to become." The German word for "to become" is **werden** *(<u>vehr</u>-den)*.

- ✔ **Bowle** *(boh-le)*: This noun is a mixed drink of fruits and alcohol and not a "bowl," which in German, is **Schüssel** *(<u>shuu</u>-sel)* (the one you put food into) or **Kugel** *(<u>koo</u>-gel)* (sports-type ball).

- ✔ **brav** *(brahf)*: This word means "well behaved" and not "brave." The German word for "brave" is **tapfer** *(<u>tâp</u>-fer)*.

- ✔ **Brief** *(breef)*: This word is a noun and means "letter" and not "brief." The German translation for the adjective "brief" is **kurz** *(kûrts)*, and, for the noun, **Auftrag** *(owf-trahgk)* or **Unterlagen** *(ûn-ter-lah-gen)*.

✔ **Chef** *(shêf)*: This one is the guy you take orders from, your boss or principal, and not the guy who's in charge of the cooking. The German word for "chef" is **Küchenchef** *(kuu-Hên-shêf)* or **Chefkoch** *(shêf-kôH)*.

✔ **eventuell** *(eh-vên-too-êl)*: This one means "possibly" and not "eventually," which would be **schließlich** *(shlees-lîH)* in German.

✔ **genial** *(gê-nee-ahl)*: This adjective describes an idea or person "of genius" and has nothing to do with "genial." The German word for "genial" is **heiter** *(hy-ter)*.

✔ **Kind** *(kînt)*: This one is the German word for "child" and has nothing to do with the English "kind," which would be **nett** *(nêt)* or **liebenswürdig** *(lee-bens-vuur-digk)* in German.

✔ **Komfort** *(kôm-fohr)*: This word means "amenity" — describing something that is comfortable — and not "comfort." The German word for "comfort" is **Trost** *(trohst)*.

✔ **Most** *(môst)*: This German word means a young wine (or juice). The German word for the English "most" is **das meiste** *(dâs my-ste)*. For example, you would say **die meisten Leute** *(die my-sten loy-te)* (most people).

✔ **ordinär** *(ôr-dî-nêr)*: This word means "vulgar" rather than "ordinary." The German word for "ordinary" is **normal** *(nôr-mahl)* or **gewöhnlich** *(ge-vuohn-lîH)*.

✔ **pathetisch** *(pâ-teh-tîsh)*: This one means "overly emotional" and not "pathetic," which, in German, is **jämmerlich** *(yê-mer-lîH)* or **armselig** *(ârm-zeh-ligk)*.

✔ **Provision** *(prô-vî-zîohn)*: The meaning of this word is "commission" and not "provision." The German word for "provision" is **Vorsorge** *(fohr-zôr-ge)* or **Versorgung** *(fêr-zôr-gungk)*.

✔ **psychisch** (*psuu-Hĩsh*): This word means "psychological" and not "psychic." The German translation for "psychic" is **Medium** (*meh-dĩ-um*) (if you mean the person) or **telepathisch** (*têle-pah-tĩsh*).

✔ **See** (*zeh*): This word means "lake" or "sea." In German, the verb "to see" is **sehen** (*seh-hên*).

✔ **sensibel** (*zen-zee-bel*): The meaning of this word is "sensitive" and not "sensible," which translates into **vernünftig** (*fêr-nuunf-tĩgk*).

✔ **sympathisch** (*zuum-pah-tĩsh*): This word means "nice" and not "sympathetic." The German word for "sympathetic" is **mitfühlend** (*mĩt-fuu-lent*).

Lenders and borrowers

The English language has adopted a few German words and retained their meaning with a different pronunciation, such as **Kindergarten** (*kĩn-der-gâr-ten*) (**Garten** is the German word for garden), **Zeitgeist** (*tsyt-gyst*), **Leitmotiv** (*lyt-mô-teef*), and **Angst** (*ângst*) — a term that lately has become quite fashionable.

However, many more English words have made their way into the German language. Sometimes, the combination of English and German leads to quite remarkable linguistic oddities. For example, you may hear **das ist gerade in/out** (*dãs ĩst gê-rah-de in/out*) (that's in/out right now) or **check das mal ab** (*check dãs mahl âp*) (check that out).

The following English words are commonly used in German:

✔ **der Boss**

✔ **das Business**

✔ **die City**

✔ **cool**

✔ **das Design**

- ✔ der Dress Code
- ✔ das Event
- ✔ Fashion (used without article)
- ✔ das Feeling
- ✔ das Fast Food
- ✔ Hi
- ✔ hip
- ✔ der Hit
- ✔ das Jet Set
- ✔ der Job
- ✔ das Jogging
- ✔ der Manager
- ✔ das Marketing
- ✔ Okay
- ✔ das Outing
- ✔ overdressed/underdressed
- ✔ die Party
- ✔ das Ranking (mostly sports)
- ✔ das Shopping
- ✔ die Show/Talkshow
- ✔ das Steak
- ✔ der Thriller
- ✔ das Understatement
- ✔ Wow

Here are a few phrases using these English words in German:

- ✔ **Hi, wie geht's? Wie ist der neue Job?** *(hi, vee gêhts? vee îst dehr noye job)* (Hi. How are you? How is the new job?)

- ✔ **Super! Ich mache Marketing und mein Boss ist total nett.** *(super! îH mâ-He marketing ûnt myn*

>   boss *îst <u>tô</u>-tahl nêt*) (Super! I'm doing marketing
>   and my boss is totally nice.)
>
> ✔ **Warst Du in der City?** *(vahrst doo în dehr city)*
>   (Have you been downtown?)

And finally, German uses a few "fake" English terms.
These terms wouldn't be used in the same context in
the English language. For example, the German word
for a mobile phone is **"Handy,"** and a **"Party Service"**
is a company that caters parties and public events.

Mouthing Off: Basic Pronunciation

The key to pronouncing a foreign language is forget-
ting your fear of sounding awkward and never getting
it right. To master the language, you need to know the
basic rules of pronunciation and concentrate on small
units, which can gradually be expanded — from
sounds to words and sentences. The rest is practice,
practice, practice.

The German alphabet has the same number of letters
as the English one, 26. However, many of the letters
are pronounced differently than their English counter-
parts. The good news is that German words are pronounced exactly as they are. Here's the German
alphabet:

a *(ah)*	**i** *(ih)*
b *(beh)*	**j** *(yot)*
c *(tseh)*	**k** *(kah)*
d *(deh)*	**l** *(ell)*
e *(eh)*	**m** *(em)*
f *(eff)*	**n** *(en)*
g *(geh)*	**o** *(oh)*
h *(hah)*	**p** *(peh)*

q *(koo)*	**v** *(fow)*
r *(err)*	**w** *(veh)*
s *(ess)*	**x** *(eks)*
t *(teh)*	**y** *(üppsilon)*
u *(ooh)*	**z** *(tset)*

Pronouncing vowels

In German, vowels *(a, e, i, o,* and *u)* can have long, drawn-out vowel sounds or shorter vowel sounds. Luckily, a few general rules do apply:

- ✔ A vowel is long when it's followed by an "h," as in **Stahl** *(shtahl)* (steel).

- ✔ A vowel is long when a single consonant follows it, as in **Tag** *(tahgk)* (day).

- ✔ A vowel is long when it's doubled, as in **Teer** *(tehr)* (tar) or **Aal** *(ahl)* (eel).

- ✔ In general, a vowel is short when two or more consonants follow it, as in **Tanne** *(tâ-ne)* (fir tree).

Table 1-2 gives you an idea of how to pronounce German vowels by providing you with examples and a phonetic script — the letter combinations that serve as the English equivalent of the German letter's pronunciation.

In this book's phonetic script, *diacritics* (the little "hats" on letters) (for example, ê) indicate that a vowel sound is short.

Table 1-2		Pronouncing German Vowels	
German Letter	**Symbol**	**As in English**	**German Word**
a (long)	ah	father	**Laden** *(lah-den)* (store)
a (short)	â	dark	**Platz** *(plâts)* (place)

German Letter	Symbol	As in English	German Word
e (long)	eh	beige	**Leben** *(leh-ben)* (life)
e (short/ stressed)	ê	let	**Bett** *(bêt)* (bed)
e (short/ unstressed)	e (second e)	elevator	**Lachen** *(lâ-Hen)* (laughter)
i (long)	ee	deer	**Ritus** *(ree-tûs)* (rite)
i (short)	î	winter	**Milch** *(mîlH)* (milk)
o (long)	oh	foe	**Lob** *(lohp)* (praise)
o (short)	ô	lottery	**Motte** *(mô-te)* (moth)
u (long)	oo	lunar	**Tube** *(too-be)*
u (short)	û	look	**Rum** *(rûm)* (rum)

Pronounce the German vowel "i" (long and short) like the English sound "ee"!

Pronouncing umlauts

You may have seen those pesky little dots that sometimes appear over vowels in German words. They're called **Umlaute** *(ûm-low-te)* (umlauts). They slightly alter the sound of a vowel, as outlined in Table 1-3.

Nouns sometimes acquire an umlaut in their plural form.

Table 1-3		Pronouncing Vowels with Umlauts	
German Letter	*Symbol*	*As in English*	*German Word*
ä (long)	ai	hair	**nächste** *(naiH-ste)* (next)
ä (short)	ê	let	**Bäcker** *(bê-ker)* (baker)
ö	uo	learn	**hören** *(huo-ren)* (hear)
ü	uu	lure	**Tür** *(tuur)* (door)

Pronouncing diphthongs

Diphthongs are combinations of two vowels in one syllable (as in the English "lie"), and the German language has quite a few of them, as shown in Table 1-4.

Table 1-4		Pronouncing German Diphthongs	
German Diphthongs	*Symbol*	*As in English*	*German Word*
ai	y	cry	**Mais** *(mys)* (corn)
au	ow	now	**laut** *(lowt)* (noisy)
au	oh	restaurant	**Restaurant** *(rês-toh-rong)* (restaurant)
äu / eu	oy	boy	**Häuser** *(hoy-zer)* (houses) / **Leute** *(loy-te)* (people)
ei	ay / y	cry	**ein** *(ayn)* (a) / **mein** *(myn)* (my)
ie	ee	deer	**Liebe** *(lee-be)* (love)

Pronouncing consonants

You may be relieved to discover that the sounds of German consonants aren't as unfamiliar as those of the vowels. In fact, German consonants are either pronounced like their English equivalents or like other English consonants. Well, there are a couple of oddities and exceptions, which we show you later.

Pronounce the letters **f, h, k, l, m, n, p, t,** and **x** the same as in English.

Although the German "r" is represented as "r" in the phonetic script of this book, it's pronounced differently. In German, you don't roll the "r." To make the sound, position your tongue as if you want to make the "r" sound, but instead of rolling the tip of your tongue off your palate, leave the tongue straight and try to produce the sound in the back of your throat!

Table 1-5 tells you how to pronounce the rest of the German consonants.

Table 1-5		Pronouncing German Consonants	
German Letter	**Symbol**	**As in English**	**German Word**
b	p	up / Peter	**Abfahrt** *(âp-<u>fahrt</u>)* (departure)
b	b	bright	**Bild** *(bîlt)* (image, picture)
c	k	cat	**Café** *(kâ-<u>feh</u>)* (café)
c	ts	tsar	**Celsius** *(<u>tsêl</u>-zî-ûs)* (Celsius)
c	tsh	cello	**Cello** *(<u>tshê</u>-loh)*
d	t	"t" as in moot	**blind** *(blînt)* (blind)

(continued)

Table 1-5 *(continued)*

German Letter	Symbol	As in English	German Word
d	d	do	**durstig** *(dûr-stigk)* (thirsty)
g	gg	go	**geben** *(geh-ben)* (give)
g	gk	lag	**Tag** *(tahgk)* (day)
j	y	es	**ja** *(yah)* (yes)
qu	kv	quick	**Quatsch** *(kvâtsh)* (nonsense)
s (beginning of a word)	z	zoo	**sieben** *(zee-ben)* (seven)
s (middle/end of a word)	s	sit	**Haus** *(hows)* (house)
v	f	"f" as in fire	**Vogel** *(foh-gel)* (bird)
v	v	velvet	**Vase** *(vah-ze)* (vase)
w	v	vice	**Wald** *(vâlt)* (forest)
y	y	yes	**Yoga** *(yoh-gâ)* (yoga)
y	uu	syllable	**System** *(zuus-tehm)* (system)
z	ts	"ts" as in tsar	**Zahl** *(tsahl)* (number)

Identifying a new letter: ß

In written German, you come across a letter, **ß** *(ês-tsêt)*, which is a combination of the letters **s** *(ês)* and **z** *(tsêt)* and is pronounced as a sharp "s." It's considered a single consonant but isn't an additional letter of the alphabet.

The German language used to have quite a few words that were spelled either with "ss" or "ß" (the sound is identical) and it was tricky to get the spelling right. German has recently undergone a spelling reform that solved this problem. Here's the scoop:

- ✔ After a long vowel, the sharp "s" is spelled "ß" — for example in **Fuß** *(foos)* (foot).

- ✔ After a short vowel, the sharp "s" is spelled "ss" — for example in **Fass** *(fâs)* (barrel).

Switzerland doesn't use the ß at all. Instead, the Swiss always spell words with the double "ss."

Pronouncing combinations of consonants

The German language has a few combinations of consonants that don't occur in the English language. Most of them are easy to pronounce, with the exception of "ch," which is unfamiliar to the English tongue.

The letter combination **ch** has absolutely no equivalent in English. It's kind of a gargling hiss and is represented by a capital "H" in the phonetic script in this book.

Try to approximate this sound by starting with the way you pronounce the letter "h" in the beginning of the word human and then drawing out and emphasizing the "h." The "ch" sound is produced at the same place in the back of your throat as the "k" sound. But instead of rolling your tongue in the back of your mouth — as you do when you pronounce a "k" — you have to lower it and bring it forward to your front teeth. If you practice it a little, you shouldn't have problems pronouncing the words **ich** *(îH)* (I) and **vielleicht** *(fee-lyHt)* (perhaps). (Yes, it does sound a bit like your cat when she has a hairball.)

The good news is that there are a couple of words where "ch" is simply pronounced as a "k," for example in **Wachs** *(vâks)* (wax) or **Lachs** *(lâks)* (salmon).

If the "ch" is preceded by a bright vowel (e, i, ü, ö, a) and not followed by an "s," pronounce the "ch" as in **ich** *(îH)*, which is more open and happens closer to the teeth. If the "ch" is preceded by a dark vowel (a, o, u), the "ch" is pronounced like the "hairball" example earlier in this section.

Table 1-6 shows you how to pronounce some other common consonant combinations.

Table 1-6		Pronouncing ck, sch, sp, and st	
German Letter	*Symbol*	*As in English*	*German Word*
ck	k	check	**Dreck** *(drêk)* (dirt)
sch	sh	shut	**Tisch** *(tîsh)* (table)
sp	shp	"sh" as in shut and "p" as in people	**spät** *(shpait)* (late)
st (beginning of a word)	sht	"sh" as in shut and "t" as in table	**Stadt** *(shtât)* (city)
st (middle/ end of a word)	st	stable	**Last** *(lâst)* (burden)
tsch	tsh	switch	**Deutsch** *(doytsh)* (German)

The German language doesn't have a sound for the English "th" sound. The "h" is either silent, as in the words **Theorie** *(teh-oh-ree)* (theory) or **Theologie** *(teh-oh-lô-gee)* (theology). Or, the letters "t" and "h" are

pronounced separately, as in the words
Rasthaus *(râst-hows)* (inn) or **Basthut** *(bâst-hoot)* (straw hat).

Using Popular Expressions

German has many *idioms*, expressions typical of a language and culture that don't really make sense if translated word for word. Here are a few:

- ✔ **Ein Fisch auf dem Trockenen** *(ayn fĭsh owf dehm trôk-nen)* (a fish on the dry, meaning: "a fish out of water.")

- ✔ **Es regnet Bindfäden** *(ês rehgk-nêt bĭnt-fê-den)* (It's raining twine, meaning: "It's raining cats and dogs.")

- ✔ **Das macht den Braten (den Kohl) nicht fett.** *(dâs mâHt dehn brah-ten [dehn kohl] nĭHt fêt)* (That doesn't make the roast [the cabbage] fat, meaning: "That won't make much difference" or "That won't help.")

- ✔ **den Braten riechen** *(dehn brah-ten ree-Hen)* (to smell the roast, meaning: "to get wind of something")

Apart from these idioms, you can easily master some of the following frequently used German expressions:

- ✔ **Prima!** *(pree-mah)* (Great!)

- ✔ **Klasse!** *(klâ-se)* (Great!)

- ✔ **Toll!** *(tôl)* (Great!)

- ✔ **Einverstanden.** *(ayn-fêr-shtân-den)* (Agreed./Okay.)

- ✔ **Geht in Ordnung.** *(geht ĭn ôrt-nûngk)* (I'll do it.)

- ✔ **Wird gemacht.** *(vîrt ge-mâHt)* (Okay./Will be done.)

- ✔ **Keine Frage.** *(ky-ne frah-ge)* (No question.)

- ✔ **Macht nichts.** *(mâHt nĭHts)* (Never mind. /That's okay.)

- ✔ **Nicht der Rede wert.** *(nîHt dehr <u>reh</u>-de vehrt)* (Don't mention it.)

- ✔ **Schade!** *(<u>shah</u>-de)* (Too bad!)

- ✔ **So ein Pech!** *(zoh ayn pêH)* (Bad luck!)

- ✔ **Viel Glück!** *(feel gluuk)* (Good luck!)

- ✔ **Prost!** *(prohst)* (Cheers!)

Chapter 2

Grammar on a Diet: Just the Basics

. . . .

In This Chapter

▶ Constructing simple sentences

▶ Forming questions

▶ Introducing regular and irregular verbs

▶ The tenses: past, present, and future

▶ Making a case for cases

. . . .

*G*rammar can be a bit intimidating, but it doesn't have to be. As soon as you get the hang of some basic rules, you can use grammar without even thinking about it — just like the natives. Go with the flow, keep your cool, and you'll be okay.

Looking at the Types of Words

To construct a simple sentence in German, you need a certain number of building elements: nouns, adjectives, verbs, and adverbs are the most important types of words.

Nouns

All German nouns have genders. They can be masculine, feminine, or neuter. And most of them can be singular or plural.

Nouns usually appear in the company of articles like
"the" or "a." The best way to familiarize yourself with
the gender of a German noun is to remember the
word together with its definite article, which indicates
the word's gender. The English definite article "the" is
transformed into

- ✔ **For masculine nouns:** You use **der** *(dehr)* (masculine). For example, **der Garten** *(dehr gârtn)*
  (the garden).

- ✔ **For feminine nouns:** You use **die** *(dee)* (feminine). For example, **die Tür** *(dee tuur)* (the
  door).

- ✔ **For neutral nouns:** You use **das** *(dâs)* (neuter).
  For example, **das Haus** *(dâs hows)* (the house).

The English indefinite articles "a," "an," and "some"
are transformed into

- ✔ **For masculine nouns:** You use **ein** *(ayn)*. For
  example, **ein Name** *(ayn nah-me* (a name).

- ✔ **For feminine nouns:** You add an *e* to **ein,**
  making **eine** *(ay-ne)*. For example, **eine Firma**
  (ay-ne fir-mah) (a company).

- ✔ **For neuter nouns:** You also use **ein.** For example, **ein Büro** *(ayn buu-roh)* (an office).

In the plural, everything is comparatively easy. The
definite article for all plural words is **die** *(dee)*. And,
as in English, the indefinite article "a" just vanishes in
the plural.

Two other tidbits to remember about
German nouns:

- ✔ They always start with a capital letter.
- ✔ They form very long compounds.

However, if you can recognize the components that
make up a long noun, you can guess the meaning of
many of these compounds without looking them up. A
good example is the word **Postleitzahl** *(pôst-lyt-tsahl)*.
It consists of the components **Post** *(pôst)* (postal

service), **leit** *(lyt)* (guide), and **Zahl** *(tsahl)* (number), combining to mean a "mail guiding number" — a zip code.

Adjectives

Adjectives describe nouns. In German, adjectives have different endings depending on the gender, case (more about that later in this chapter), and number (singular or plural) of the noun they accompany, and depending on whether a definite article, indefinite article, or no article at all accompanies the adjective.

The following are the endings for adjectives accompanied by a definite article: We use the adjectives **schön** *(shuon)* (beautiful), **weiß** *(vys)* (white), **groß** *(grohs)* (large), and **klein** *(klyn)* (small) as examples. The adjective endings for the subject case (or nominative case) appear in italics:

- ✔ **der schön***e* **Garten** *(dehr shuo-ne gâr-tn)* (the beautiful garden)
- ✔ **die weiß***e* **Tür** *(dee vy-sse tuur)* (the white door)
- ✔ **das klein***e* **Haus** *(dâss kly-ne hows)* (the small house)
- ✔ **die groß***en* **Häuser** *(dee groh-ssn hoi-zer)* (the large houses)

The following are the endings for adjectives accompanied by an indefinite article:

- ✔ **ein schön***er* **Garten** *(ayn shuo-ner gâr-tn)* (a beautiful garden)
- ✔ **eine weiß***e* **Tür** *(ay-ne vy-sse tuur)* (a white door)
- ✔ **ein klein***es* **Haus** *(ayn kly-nes hows)* (a small house)
- ✔ **groß***e* **Häuser** *(groh-sse hoi-zer)* (large houses)

The following are the endings for adjectives when used alone:

✔ **schön*er* Garten** *(shuo-ner gâr-tn)* (beautiful garden)

✔ **weiße Tür** *(vy-sse tuur)* (white door)

✔ **klein*es* Haus** *(kly-nes hows)* (small house)

✔ **groß*e* Häuser** *(groh-sse hoi-zer)* (large houses)

If a definite article doesn't precede the adjective, the adjective takes the ending as if used with an indefinite article.

Verbs

Verbs express actions or states. The person doing the action is its subject, and the verb always adjusts its ending to the subject. For example, the door opens, but the doors open, and so on.

The verb form that has no marking to indicate its subject or a tense (past, present, or future) is called the *infinitive.* German infinitives usually have the ending **-en,** as in **lachen** *(lâ-Hen)* (to laugh). Some verbs end in **-n, -rn,** or **-ln.** In English the infinitive is usually preceded by "to."

Regular verbs don't change their stem when you conjugate them, and their endings are always the same. Here are the endings of the regular verb **sagen** *(sah-ghen)* (to say) in the present tense, tagged on to its stem **sag-:**

Ich(I) **sag-e** (I say)

Du sag-st (you [informal] say)

Sie sag-en (you [formal] say)

er, sie, es sag-t (he/she/it says)

wir sag-en (we say)

ihr sag-t (you [informal, plural] say)

Sie sag-en (you [formal, plural] say)

sie sag-en (they say)

Seems easy, doesn't it? But there are — as usual — some exceptions to the rule. When the verb stem ends in **m**, **n**, **d**, or **t**, you have to insert an **e** before the ending in the **du**, **er/sie/es**, and **ihr** constructions:

> **du atm-e-st** (you [informal] breathe)
>
> **er arbeit-e-t** (he works)
>
> **ihr bad-e-t** (you [informal, plural] bathe)

Why do they do that? Try to pronounce "atmst," and you'll figure out why.

Adverbs

Adverbs accompany verbs or adjectives and describe them. In English, most adverbs end with -ly (as in: I *quickly* put my green socks on). In German, adverbs are most often adjectives with unmodified endings.

Figuring Out Simple Sentence Construction

Nouns, verbs, adjectives, and adverbs usually aren't thrown together haphazardly; words are arranged into sentences according to certain rules.

Arranging words in the right order

"Normal" word order in German is much like English word order. The subject comes first, followed by the verb, followed by the rest of the sentence. Unless you have reason not to, use the following word order.

Subject	Verb	Object
Meine Freundin	**hat**	**einen VW-Bus**
<u>my</u>-ne <u>froyn</u>-dîn	hât	<u>ay</u>-nen fow-<u>veh</u> bûs
My girlfriend	has	a VW van

Independent clauses: Putting the verb in second place

One of the most important things to remember is the verb placement in a German sentence. In independent clauses, like the one in the preceding section, and in the following sentence, the verb is always in second place, no matter what.

> **Meine Freundin fährt nach Dänemark.** (_my-ne froyn-dîn fehrt nâH deh-ne-mârk_) (My girlfriend drives to Denmark.)

How about adding some more information?

> **Meine Freundin fährt morgen nach Dänemark.** (_my-ne froyn-dîn fehrt môrgn nâH deh-ne-mârk_) (My girlfriend goes to Denmark tomorrow.)

Again, the verb is in second place.

What happens if the sentence starts with **morgen** (_môrgn_) (tomorrow)?

> **Morgen fährt meine Freundin nach Dänemark.**

Morgen is in first place, and the verb has to be in second place, so the subject follows the verb. Technically, this is called _inversion of the verb._ All it means is that verb and subject switch places, and it happens whenever anything other than the subject is in the first place of a sentence. Generally, you change the word order to shift emphasis.

Dependent clauses: Pushing the verb to the end

The examples used so far in this section have all been independent, stand-alone sentences, but sometimes several statements combine to form a more complex structure:

> **Meine Freundin sagt, dass sie nach Dänemark fährt.** (_my-ne froyn-dîn zahgt, dâs zee nâH deh-ne-mârk fehrt_) (My girlfriend says that she goes to Denmark.)

The main verb **sagt** *(zahgt)* (says) is in second place where you would expect it, but the verb in the second, dependent clause introduced by **dass** *(dâs)* (that) goes all the way to the end. That happens in all dependent clauses.

Dependent clauses typically start with (subordinating) conjunctions (words that link sentences) like **dass, weil,** and **damit** *(dâs, vyl, dâ-mît)* (that, because, so that), and they always end with the verb.

Forming questions

The German word order for asking questions corresponds nicely to the English word order for questions. You begin with a verb and the subject follows.

Fährt deine Freundin nach Dänemark? *(fehrt dy-ne froyn-dîn nâH deh-ne-mârk)* (Is your girlfriend going to Denmark?)

Hat deine Freundin einen VW-Bus? *(hât dy-ne froyn-dîn ay-nen fow-veh-bûs)* (Does your girlfriend have a VW van?)

Note that you don't have to worry about the verb "do" in German when forming questions.

Another way to elicit information is to use the question words:

wer? *(vehr)* (who?)

was? *(vâs)* (what?)

wo? *(voh)* (where?)

wann? *(vân)* (when?)

wie? *(vee)* (how?)

warum? *(vah-rûm)* (why?)

was für ein(e/en) . . .? *(vâs fuur ayn/e/en)* (what kind of . . .?)

welche/r/s . . .? *(vêl-He/r/s?)* (which?)

When forming questions with these words, the verb goes in its usual place — second:

- ✔ **Wer fährt nach Dänemark?** *(vehr fehrt nâH <u>deh</u>-ne-mârk)* (Who goes to Denmark?)

- ✔ **Was für ein Auto hat deine Freundin?** *(vâs fuur ayn <u>ow</u>-tô hât <u>dy</u>-ne <u>froyn</u>-dîn)* (What kind of car does your girlfriend have?)

- ✔ **Wann fährt sie nach Dänemark?** *(vân fehrt zee nâH <u>deh</u>-ne-mârk)* (When does she go to Denmark?)

- ✔ **Wie kommt deine Freundin nach Dänemark?** *(vee kômt <u>dy</u>-ne <u>froyn</u>-dîn nâH <u>deh</u>-ne-mârk)* (How does your girlfriend get to Denmark?)

The Tenses: Present, Past, and Future

"Tense" is the grammarians' preferred word for "time." Depending when the action that you're talking about is taking place, you pick a tense. The ways to look at the concept of time differ slightly from one culture and language to the next, so the way tenses are used sometimes differs, too.

Looking at the present

The present tense is a very useful tense in German. You can get a long way with just this one tense. The German present tense corresponds to three forms in English. For example, **ich denke** *(îH <u>dên</u>-ke)* can be used as the equivalent of "I think," "I do think," or "I am thinking" in English.

The present tense describes what's happening now:

- ✔ **Was machst du gerade?** *(vâs mâHst dû ge-<u>rah</u>-de)* (What are you doing right now?)

- ✔ **Ich lese die Zeitung.** *(îH <u>leh</u>-ze dee <u>tsy</u>-tûng)* (I am reading the newspaper.)

The present tense can also describe what happens sometimes, usually, or always:

> **Freitags gehe ich oft ins Kino.** *(fry-tahgks geh-e îH ôft îns kee-nô)* (On Fridays, I often go to the movies.)

The present tense can also describe what's going to happen, particularly if the sentence has a time expression that anchors the action clearly in the future. English uses future tense to say the same statements.

> ✔ **Morgen fährt meine Freundin nach Dänemark.** *(môrgn fehrt my-ne froyn-dîn nâH deh-ne-mârk)* (Tomorrow my girlfriend will go to Denmark.)

> ✔ **Nächste Woche fahre ich nach Bremen.** *(naiH-ste vô-He fah-re îH nâH breh-men)* (Next week I am going to go to Bremen.)

And finally, the present tense can also describe what's been happening up to now:

> **Ich bin seit drei Tagen in Hamburg.** *(îH bîn zyt dry tah-gn în hâm-bûrg)* (I have been in Hamburg for three days.)

Note that English uses present perfect tense to say the same type of thing.

Talking about the past: Using the perfect tense

Perfect tense is the main past tense used in spoken German. It's very versatile: You can use it to talk about most actions and situations in the past. Contrast this with the English perfect tense (I have gone, I have read, and so on), which can only be used in certain specific contexts. For example, "I have seen Anna last week" would be incorrect English, but **Ich habe Anna letzte Woche gesehen** *(îH hah-be ânâ lêts-te vô-He ge-zehn)* is a correct German statement.

To form the perfect tense, you need two things:

✔ The appropriate present-tense form of either **haben** *(hah-ben)* (to have) or **sein** *(zayn)* (to be)

✔ The past participle of the action verb, which goes at the end of the sentence

Choosing haben or sein

Whether you use **haben** or **sein** depends on which action verb you're working with. Just remember that most verbs require **haben,** but some use **sein,** and you just have to memorize which is which. Here's a quick overview of the conjugation of **haben** in the present tense:

Conjugation	Pronunciation
ich habe	îH hah-be
du hast	dû hâst
Sie haben	zee hah-bn
er / sie / es hat	ehr / zee / ês hât
wir haben	veer hah-bn
ihr habt	eer hahpt
Sie haben	zee hah-bn
sie haben	zee hah-bn

Take a look at some examples of how the verb **haben** combines with a past participle to make the perfect tense:

✔ **David hat mir geholfen.** *(dah-veed hât meer ge-hôlfn)* (David has helped me / has been helping me / helped me.)

✔ **Gestern haben wir ein Auto gekauft.** *(gês-tern hah-bn veer ayn ow-tô ge-kowft)* (Yesterday we bought a car.)

✔ **Anna hat die Zeitung gelesen.** *(ânâ hât dee tsy-tûng ge-lehzn)* (Anna has read the newspaper / read the newspaper.)

> ✔ **Ich habe den Film gesehen.** *(îH <u>hah</u>-be dehn fîlm ge-<u>zehn</u>)* (I have seen the film. / I saw the film.)

> ✔ **Hat euch der Film gefallen?** *(hât oyH dehr fîlm ge-<u>fâ</u>-len)* (Did you like the movie?)

For verbs that require **sein** in the perfect tense, the following list is an overview of the present tense forms of **sein**:

Conjugation	*Pronunciation*
ich bin	îH bîn
du bist	dû bîst
Sie sind	zee zînt
er / sie / es ist	ehr /zee / ês îst
wir sind	veer zînt
ihr seid	eer zyt
Sie sind	zee zînt
sie sind	zee zînt

Verbs in this category include the verb **sein** itself and generally verbs that indicate a change of place or a change of state. Sounds a bit theoretical? Table 2-1 shows you some common verbs that take **sein** in the perfect tense.

Table 2-1   Verbs That Use Sein in the Perfect Tense

Verb		*Past Participle*
gehen	(<u>geh</u>-en) (to go)	gegangen
fahren	(<u>fah</u>-ren) (to drive / ride / go)	gefahren
fliegen	(<u>flee</u>-gen) (to fly)	geflogen
kommen	(<u>kô</u>-men) (to come)	gekommen
laufen	(<u>low</u>-fen) (to run)	gelaufen
sein	(zyn) (to be)	gewesen

Have a look at these examples of verbs forming the present perfect tense with the present tense of **sein** and the past participle.

- ✔ **Ich bin ins Kino gegangen.** *(īH bīn īns _kee_-nô ge-_gân_-gen)* (I have gone to the movies / went to the movies.)

- ✔ **Meine Freundin ist nach Dänemark gefahren.** *(_my_-ne _froyn_-dīn īst nâH _dehne_-mârk ge-_fah_-ren)* (My girlfriend has gone to Denmark / went to Denmark.)

- ✔ **Ich bin in Hamburg gewesen.** *(īH bīn īn _hâm_-bûrg ge-_vehzn_)* (I have been to Hamburg. / I was in Hamburg.)

- ✔ **Du bist mit dem Auto gekommen.** *(dū bīst mīt dehm _ow_-tô ge-_kô_-men)* (You came by car. / You have come by car.)

- ✔ **Sie ist mit dem Zug gefahren.** *(zee īst mīt dehm tsoogk ge-_fah_-ren)* (She has gone by train. / She went by train.)

- ✔ **Wir sind letzte Woche ins Kino gegangen.** *(veer zīnt _lêts_-te _wô_-He īns _kee_-nô ge-_gân_-gen)* (We went to the movies last week.)

- ✔ **Seid ihr durch den Park gelaufen?** *(zyt eer dūrH dehn pârk ge-_low_-fen)* (Have you run through the park? / Did you run through the park?)

- ✔ **Sie sind gestern im Theater gewesen.** *(zee zīnt _gês_-tern īm teh-_ah_-ter ge-_veh_-zen)* (They were at the theater yesterday.)

If the sentence is a question, the correct form of **haben** (or **sein**) appears as the first word of the sentence. If your sentence is a straightforward statement, it appears as the second word of the sentence.

Forming the past participle

The past participle is a form you may want to learn with each new verb. However, a few rules can make life easier. In order to apply these rules, you need to know which category the verb in question falls into: weak and strong verbs.

Weak verbs (ones who need to hit the gym), also known as regular verbs, form the largest group of German verbs. When forming the past participle of a weak verb, use the following formula:

ge + **verb stem** (the infinitive minus **-en**) + **(e)t** = **past participle**

Look at how the formula plays out on the common verb **fragen** *(frah-gen)* (to ask):

ge + **frag** + **t** = **gefragt** *(gê-frahgkt)*

For some words, you have to add an **-et** instead of **-t** so that you can actually pronounce the work. For example, **reden** *(reh-den)* (to talk):

ge + **red** + **et** = **geredet** *(gê-reh-dêt)*

Other verbs, the so-called strong verbs (the ones with hard pecs and chiseled abs), also known as irregular verbs, follow a different pattern. They add **ge-** in the beginning and **-en** at the end. Forming the past participle of a strong verb entails the following:

ge + **verb stem** (the infinitive minus **-en**) + **en** = **past participle**

The verb **kommen** *(kô-men)* (to come) is a good example for this:

ge + **komm** + **en** = **gekommen** *(gê-kômn)*

Some strong verbs change their verb stem when forming a past participle. For example, a stem vowel, and sometimes even a stem consonant, can change.

The verb **helfen** *(hêl-fen)* (to help) changes its stem vowel:

ge + **holf** + **en** = **geholfen** *(gê-hôl-fn)*

The verb **gehen** (*geh-en*) (to go) changes a vowel and a consonant!

ge + **gang** + **en** = **gegangen** (*gê-gângn*)

> **Gehen,** a verb indicating a change of place, is one of the verbs conjugated (or used) with **sein.** All the verbs conjugated with **sein** are strong verbs. So you need to remember a vowel and possibly a consonant change for each of them. Memorize the past participle whenever you pick up a new verb that's used with **sein.**

Writing about the past: Using simple past tense

Newspapers, books, and other publications use the simple past tense all the time, but it's less common in speech. One exception is the simple past tense of **sein** (*zyn*) (to be). This form is often used in preference to perfect tense in both speech and writing. Table 2-2 shows you the various forms of the simple past tense of **sein.**

Table 2-2	Simple Past Tense Forms of Sein	
Conjugation	*Pronunciation*	*Translation*
ich war	*(îH vahr)*	I was
du warst	*(dû vahrst)*	you were (informal)
Sie waren	*(zee vah-ren)*	you were (formal)
er / sie / es war	*(ehr / zee / ês vahr)*	he / she / it was
wir waren	*(veer vah-ren)*	we were
ihr wart	*(eer vahrt)*	you were (informal)
Sie waren	*(zee vah-ren)*	you were (formal)
sie waren	*(zee vah-ren)*	they were

Talking about the future

The German language doesn't use the future tense as consistently as English. In many situations, you can use the present tense instead (see "Looking at the present" in this chapter). However, the way to form future tense in German is pretty similar to English. You take the verb **werden** *(vehr-den)* (to become) and add an infinitive.

Table 2-3 shows you the forms of **werden** in the present tense.

Table 2-3	Present Tense Forms of Werden	
Conjugation	*Pronunciation*	*Translation*
ich werde	*(îH vehr-de)*	I will
du wirst	*(dû vîrst)*	you will (informal)
Sie werden	*(zee vehr-dn)*	you will (formal)
er / sie / es wird	*(ehr / zee / ês vîrt)*	he / she / it will
wir werden	*(veer vehr-dn)*	we will
ihr werdet	*(eer vehr-det)*	you will (informal)
Sie werden	*(zee vehr-dn)*	you will (formal)
sie werden	*(zee vehr-dn)*	they will

And the following examples show you how to incorporate future tense into sentences:

- ✔ **Ich werde anrufen.** *(îH vehr-de ân-roo-fen)* (I am going to call.)

- ✔ **Wir werden morgen kommen.** *(veer vehr-dn môr-gn kô-men)* (We will come tomorrow.)

- ✔ **Es wird regnen.** *(ês vîrt rehg-nen)* (It will rain. / It's going to rain.)

Getting Funky: Reflexive and Separable Verbs

German verbs have a reputation for acting a bit strangely. They do things that English verbs just don't do. For example, German verbs can go at the end of a sentence. And sometimes they split in two, with only one part of the verb going to the end of a sentence!

Right back at you: Reflexive verbs

Some German verbs need a *helper* — a pronoun in the accusative case — in order to work. The pronoun reflects back (just like a mirror) on the subject. That's why these verbs are usually called *reflexive verbs* and the pronouns are called *reflexive pronouns*.

The following table shows you the accusative reflexive pronouns.

Personal Pronoun	Reflexive Pronoun
ich	**mich** (mîH)
du	**dich** (dîH)
Sie	**sich** (zîH)
er	**sich** (zîH)
sie	**sich** (zîH)
es	**sich** (zîH)
wir	**uns** (ûns)
ihr	**euch** (oyH)
Sie	**sich** (zîH)
sie	**sich** (zîH)

The reflexive pronoun goes after the conjugated verb in a normal sentence. In a question starting with a verb, the reflexive pronoun goes after the subject. Take a look at some of these reflexive verbs and accusative reflexive pronouns (note that they're italicized) doing their thing in the following sentences:

✔ Ich *interessiere mich* für Bildhauerei. *(îH în-te-re-see-re mîH fuur bîlt-howê-ry)* (I am interested in sculpting.) Literally, this sentence translates as: I interest myself in sculpting. The subject **ich** (I) is reflected in the pronoun **mich** (myself).

✔ *Freust* du *dich* auf deinen Urlaub? *(froyst dû dîH owf dy-nen oor-lowp)* (Are you looking forward to your vacation?)

✔ Herr Grobe *meldet sich* für einen Fotokurs an. *(hêr groh-be mêl-det zîH fuur ay-nen foh-tô-kûrs ân)* (Mr. Grobe is registering for a photography class.)

✔ Herr und Frau Weber *erholen sich* im Urlaub an der Küste. *(hêr ûnt frow veh-ber êr-hoh-len zîH îm oor-lowp ân dehr kuus-te)* (Mr. and Mrs. Weber are relaxing during their vacation on the coast.)

To give you a leg up, we can tell you some of the most common reflexive verbs you may encounter. Take **sich freuen** *(zîH froy-en)* (to be happy) as an example.

Conjugation	Pronunciation
ich freue mich	îH froy-e mîH
du freust dich	dû froyst dîH
Sie freuen sich	zee froy-en zîH
er, sie, es freut sich	êr, zee, ês froyt zîH
wir freuen uns	veer froy-en ûns
ihr freut euch	eer froyt oyH
Sie freuen sich	zee froy-en zîH
sie freuen sich	zee froy-en zîH

Other very common reflexive verbs include

✔ **sich aufregen** *(zîH owf-reh-gen)* (to get excited or upset)

✔ **sich freuen auf** *(zîH froy-en owf)* (to look forward to)

- ✔ **sich freuen über** *(zîH froy-en uu-ber)* (to be glad about)

- ✔ **sich beeilen** *(zîH bê-ay-len)* (to hurry)

- ✔ **sich entscheiden** *(zîH ênt-shy-den)* (to decide)

- ✔ **sich erinnern** *(zîH êr-în-ern)* (to remember)

- ✔ **sich gewöhnen an** *(zîH ge-vuo-nen ân)* (to get used to)

- ✔ **sich interessieren für** *(zîH în-te-rê-see-ren fuur)* (to be interested in)

- ✔ **sich setzen** *(zîH zê-tsen)* (to sit down)

- ✔ **sich unterhalten** *(zîH ûn-têr-hâl-ten)* (to talk, to enjoy oneself)

- ✔ **sich verspäten** *(zîH fêr-shpeh-ten)* (to be late)

- ✔ **sich vorstellen** *(zîh fohr-shtê-len)* (to introduce oneself, to imagine)

Knowing when to separate your verbs

Many German verbs have prefixes that are actual words in their own right (like the prepositions **ab, an, um, ein,** and **aus**). These prefixes are detachable from the body of the verb when used in the present tense or simple past. The verb stem takes its expected verb ending and assumes its usual place in the sentence, while the prefix jumps to the very end of the sentence.

Take a look at the verb **ankommen** *(ân-kô-men)* (to arrive):

Der Zug kommt um 18.15 Uhr an. *(dehr tsoog kômt ûm âHt-tsehn oor fuunf-tsehn ân)* (The train arrives at 6:15 p.m.)

How do you know if a verb is separable? Two things can guide you:

> ✔ The verb needs to have a preposition serving as a prefix.
>
> ✔ The infinitive is emphasized on the first syllable.

Here are a few verbs that follow this pattern:

> ✔ **anfangen** (*<u>ân</u>-fân-gen*) (to start)
>
> ✔ **aufhören** (*<u>owf</u>-huo-ren*) (to end)
>
> ✔ **aufmachen** (*<u>owf</u>-mâ-Hen*) (to open)
>
> ✔ **zumachen** (*<u>tsû</u>-mâ-hen*) (to close)
>
> ✔ **einsteigen** (*<u>ayn</u>-shty-gen*) (to get on)
>
> ✔ **aussteigen** (*<u>ows</u>-shty-gen*) (to get off)
>
> ✔ **aufstehen** (*<u>owf</u>-shteh-en*) (to get up)
>
> ✔ **zuhören** (*<u>tsû</u>-huo-ren*) (to listen)

Putting the Language in the Right Case

All languages have ways of showing what role each noun is playing in a particular sentence. For example, who (or what) is doing what to whom. In English, you show a noun's role mainly by its position in a sentence. German speakers, on the other hand, indicate the function of a noun in a sentence mainly by adding endings to any articles or adjectives accompanying that noun (and sometimes to the noun itself).

When they're used in a sentence, nouns appear in one of four cases, depending on their role in the sentence: nominative for the subject, accusative for the direct object, dative for the indirect object, and genitive for the possessive.

Nominative case

The subject of a sentence is always in the nominative case. As a general rule, the subject is the person or thing performing the action of the verb. For example, in the sentence **Der Junge nimmt den Kuchen** *(dehr yûn-ge nîmt dehn koo-Hn)* (The boy takes the cake.), the boy is the one taking the cake: He is the subject of the sentence.

Accusative case

A sentence's direct object is always in the accusative case. The direct object is the person or thing directly affected by the action of the verb. So in the sentence **Der Junge nimmt den Kuchen** *(dehr yûn-ge nîmt dehn koo-Hn)* (The boy takes the cake.), the cake is the direct object — it's the thing that's being taken.

Dative case

The indirect object of the sentence is always in the dative case. Think of the indirect object as the person or thing indirectly affected by the action of the verb. For example, in the sentence **Der Junge gibt dem Hund den Kuchen** *(dehr yûn-ge gîpt dehm hûnt dehn koo-Hn)* (The boy gives the dog the cake.), the dog is the indirect object, the one to whom the boy gives the cake. (The cake is the direct object, the thing that is given.)

Genitive case

The genitive case indicates possession. The person or thing that possesses is in the genitive case. For example, in the phrase **der Hund des Jungen** *(dehr hûnt dês yûn-gen)* (the boy's dog), the boy possesses the dog, so it's the boy who is in the genitive case.

Why all these cases matter

Mastering the various cases is a complicated, but necessary, step when studying German. You see, the different cases make pronouns change form. And the cases also make the endings of articles and adjectives change.

How pronouns change

Pronouns are useful little words that can replace nouns. Pronouns are used instead of nouns as a way to avoid clumsy repetition. Table 2-4 shows you how the pronouns change according to case.

Table 2-4		Personal Pronouns by Case	
Nominative	**Dative**	**Accusative**	**English**
ich	mir	mich	I, to me, me
du	dir	dich	you, to you, you (singular, informal address)
Sie	Ihnen	Sie	you, to you, you (singular, formal address)
er	ihm	ihn	he, to him, him
sie	ihr	sie	she, to her, her
es	ihm	es	it, to it, it
wir	uns	uns	we, to us, us
ihr	euch	euch	you, to you, you (plural, informal address)
Sie	Ihnen	Sie	you, to you, you (plural, formal address)
sie	ihnen	sie	they, to them, them

The following is an example of the second person singular pronoun **du** appearing in the nominative, dative, and accusative cases depending on its function in a sentence.

> ✔ **Du** bist müde. *(dû bîst <u>muu</u>-de)* (You are tired.)
>   **du** = nominative
>
> ✔ Ich gebe **dir** das Buch. *(îH <u>geh</u>-be deer dâs booH)*
>   (I'm giving you the book.) **dir** = dative
>
> ✔ Ich frage **dich**. *(îH <u>frah</u>-ge dîH)* (I'm asking you.)
>   **dich** = accusative

How indefinite articles change

The endings the indefinite article **ein** *(ayn)* (a) takes
depend on whether it accompanies the subject of a
sentence (nominative), a genitive object, the direct
object (accusative), or the indirect object (dative).

Table 2-5 shows you the indefinite article **ein** being
put through the paces of the various cases.

Table 2-5	**Endings of Ein by Case**			
Gender	*Nominative*	*Genitive*	*Dative*	*Accusative*
Masculine	ein	eines	einem	einen
Feminine	eine	einer	einer	eine
Neuter	ein	eines	einem	ein

The following examples show the indefinite article **ein**
with its appropriate masculine endings in the four different cases.

> ✔ **Ein** Wagen steht auf der Straße. *(ayn <u>vah</u>-gen
>   shteht owf dehr <u>shtrah</u>-se)* (A car is standing on
>   the road.) **ein** = nominative
>
> ✔ Du liest das Buch **eines** Freundes. *(dû leest dâs
>   booH <u>ay</u>-nes <u>froyn</u>-des)* (You are reading a
>   friend's book.) **eines** = genitive
>
> ✔ Ich leihe **einem** Freund mein Auto. *(îH <u>ly</u>-he <u>ay</u>-
>   nem froynt myn <u>ow</u>-tô)* (I'm lending my car to a
>   friend.) **einem** = dative
>
> ✔ Ich habe **einen** Hund. *(îH <u>hah</u>-be <u>ay</u>-nen hûnt)*
>   (I have a dog.) **einen** = accusative

How definite articles change

The definite articles also morph depending on which case they are used in, as shown in Table 2-6.

Table 2-6	Definite Articles by Case			
Gender	*Nominative*	*Genitive*	*Dative*	*Accusative*
Masculine	der	des	dem	den
Feminine	die	der	der	die
Neuter	das	des	dem	das
Plural	die	der	den	die

The following examples show the masculine definite article **der** with its appropriate endings in the four different cases.

- ✔ **Der** Wagen steht auf der Straße. *(dehr vah-gen shteht owf dehr shtrah-se)* (The car is standing on the road.) **der** = nominative

- ✔ Du liest das Buch **des** Freundes. *(dû leest dâs booH dês froyn-dês)* (You are reading the friend's book.) **des** = genitive

- ✔ Ich leihe **dem** Freund mein Auto. *(îH ly-he dehm froynt myn ow-tô)* (I'm lending my car to the friend.) **dem** = dative

- ✔ Ich habe **den** Hund. *(îH hah-be dehn hûnt)* (I have the dog.) **den** = accusative

How possessives change

Possessive pronouns establish ownership. They mark the difference between what belongs to you ("your book"), what belongs to me ("my book"), and so on. Here is a run-through of the forms for the different persons:

- ✔ **mein** *(myn)* (my)
- ✔ **dein** *(dyn)* (your) (informal address)

✔ **Ihr** *(eer)* (your) (formal address)

✔ **sein / ihr / sein** *(zyn / eer / zyn)* (his / her / its)

✔ **unser** *(ūn-zer)* (our)

✔ **euer** *(oy-er)* (your) (informal address)

✔ **Ihr** *(eer)* (your) (formal address)

✔ **ihr** *(eer)* (their)

Table 2-7 presents all the forms in the singular of a sample possessive, **mein** *(myn)*. The other possessives take the same endings. These endings may look familiar; they're the same as those for the indefinite article **ein.**

Table 2-7	**Possessive Endings by Case**			
Gender	*Nominative*	*Genitive*	*Dative*	*Accusative*
Masculine	mein	meines	meinem	meinen
Feminine	meine	meiner	meiner	meine
Neuter	mein	meines	meinem	mein

How adjective endings change

Adjectives accompanying nouns change their endings depending on the role of the noun in the sentence, as shown in Table 2-8.

Table 2-8	**Endings for Adjectives Preceded by the Definite and Indefinite Articles**			
Gender	*Nominative*	*Genitive*	*Dative*	*Accusative*
Masculine	e/er	en/en	en/en	en/en
Feminine	e/e	en/en	en/en	e/e
Neuter	e/es	en/en	en/en	e/es

To illustrate the endings shown in Table 2-8, we provide examples of nouns accompanied by an adjective and the definite or indefinite article, respectively, in Table 2-9 and Table 2-10.

Table 2-9	Examples of Adjective Endings Preceded by Indefinite Articles			
Gender	**Nominative**	**Genitive**	**Dative**	**Accusative**
Masculine	ein schöner Garten	eines schönen Gartens	einem schönen Garten	einen schönen Garten
Feminine	eine weiße Tür	einer weißen Tür	einer weißen Tür	eine weiße Tür
Neuter	ein kleines Haus	eines kleinen Hauses	einem kleinen Haus	ein kleines Haus

Table 2-10	Examples of Adjective Endings Preceded by Definite Articles			
Gender	**Nominative**	**Genitive**	**Dative**	**Accusative**
Masculine	der schöne Garten	des schönen Gartens	dem schönen Garten	den schönen Garten
Feminine	die weiße Tür	der weißen Tür	der weißen Tür	die weiße Tür
Neuter	das kleine Haus	des kleinen Hauses	dem kleinen Haus	das kleine Haus

Getting Formal or Informal

Germans tend to have a reputation for being formal, an impression that might, at least to some extent, be created by the distinction they make between different ways of saying "you." In German, you use either the formal **Sie** *(zee)* or the informal **du** *(dū)* — depending on whom you're addressing.

Observing the distinction between the two forms of "you" is quite important: People will consider you impolite if you use the informal way of addressing them in a situation that asks for more formality.

In general, you use the formal **Sie** when addressing somebody you've never met, an official, a superior, or someone who is older than you. As you get to know somebody better, you may switch to **du.** There even is a verb for using the informal "you" — **duzen** *(dū-tsen).* **Wir duzen uns.** *(veer dū-tsen ūnts)* means "We are using the informal you."

However, the German language doesn't have any fixed rules and it has a lot of exceptions when it comes to using **du** or **Sie.** For example, say that you're traveling in Germany and one of your German friends takes you to a party. Even though you haven't met any of the people there, they may just address you with **du,** which is particularly true if they're younger, and they'll probably expect you to address them with **du.** Basically, it all depends on the environment. In some offices, coworkers address each other with **du,** and in others, everybody sticks to the formal **Sie.**

If you're the least bit unsure of whether to use **du** or **Sie,** use **Sie** until the person you're addressing asks you to use **du** or addresses you with **du.**

Chapter 3

Numerical Gumbo: Counting of All Kinds

N*umbers make the world go round, or is that money? Well, it's probably both. This chapter gives you a rundown on number and money phrases and also shows you how to tell time and navigate the months of the year.

1, 2, 3: Cardinal Numbers

Cardinal numbers are important when talking about amounts, telling time, or exchanging money.

0 null *(nūl)*

1 eins *(ayns)*

2 zwei *(tsvy)*

3 drei *(dry)*

4 vier *(feer)*

5 fünf *(fuunf)*

6 sechs *(zêks)*

7 sieben *(zeebn)*

8 acht *(āHt)*

9 neun *(noyn)*

10 zehn *(tsehn)*

11 elf *(êlf)*

12 zwölf *(tsvuolf)*

13 dreizehn *(<u>dry</u>-tsehn)*

14 vierzehn *(<u>feer</u>-tsehn)*

15 fünfzehn *(<u>fuunf</u>-tsehn)*

16 sechzehn *(<u>zêH</u>-tsehn)*

17 siebzehn *(<u>zeeb</u>-tsehn)*

18 achtzehn *(<u>āH</u>-tsehn)*

19 neunzehn *(<u>noyn</u>-tsehn)*

20 zwanzig *(<u>tsvân</u>-tsîgk)*

21 einundzwanzig *(<u>ayn</u>-ûnt-tsvân-tsîgk)*

22 zweiundzwanzig *(<u>tsvy</u>-ûnt-tzvân-tsîgk)*

23 dreiundzwanzig *(<u>dry</u>-ûnt-tsvân-tsîgk)*

24 vierundzwanzig *(<u>feer</u>-ûnt-tsvân-tsîgk)*

25 fünfundzwanzig *(<u>fuunf</u>-ûnt-tsvân-tsîgk)*

30 dreissig *(<u>dry</u>-sîgk)*

40 vierzig *(<u>fîr</u>-tsîgk)*

50 fünfzig *(<u>fuunf</u>-tsîgk)*

60 sechzig *(<u>sêH</u>-tsîgk)*

70 siebzig *(<u>zeep</u>-tsîgk)*

80 achtzig *(<u>āH</u>-tsîgk)*

90 neunzig *(<u>noyn</u>-tsîgk)*

100 hundert *(<u>hûn</u>-dert)*

200 zweihundert *(<u>tsvy</u>-hûn-dert)*

300 dreihundert *(<u>dry</u>-hûn-dert)*

400 vierhundert (_feer_-hûn-dert)

500 fünfhundert (_fuunf_-hûn-dert)

1000 tausend (_tow_-zent)

You may think many of the numbers between 20 and 100 appear a bit backwards at first. Just look at 21, **einundzwanzig** (_ayn_-ûnt-tsvân-tsîgk) in German. What you actually say is "one and twenty." Just remember to stick to this pattern for all the double-digit numbers.

If you need to write out very large or very small numbers, you need commas and decimal points. The German languages uses a comma **(Komma)** where English uses a decimal point:

| English: | 20.75 | 490.99 | 3675.50 |
| German: | 20,75 | 490,99 | 3675,50 |

And this is how you say one of these numbers: 20,75 = **zwanzig Komma sieben fünf** (_tsvân_-tsîgk _kô_-mâ _zee_-bn fuunf).

You use a period in German to break up large numbers:

| English: | 100,000 dollars |
| German: | 100.000 Dollar |

The First, Second, Third, and So On

Words like second, third, and fourth are called *ordinal numbers*. They refer to a specific number in a series and answer the question "Which one?" For example, "The second on the left."

In German, you form the ordinal numbers by adding the suffix "te" to the cardinal numbers for numbers between 1 and 19 — with two exceptions, which are:

- **eins** *(ayns)* (one) / **erste** *(<u>êrs</u>-te)* (first)
- **drei** *(dry)* (three) / **dritte** *(<u>drî</u>-te)* (third)

Table 3-1 shows you how to form the ordinal numbers of numbers 1 through 10 and one example of an ordinal number formed with a "-teen" number.

Table 3-1	Sample Ordinal Numbers by Cardinal Number
Cardinal Number	*Ordinal Number*
eins (ayns) (one)	der / die / das erste (<u>êrs</u>-te) (first)
zwei (tsvy) (two)	zweite (<u>tsvy</u>-te) (second)
drei (dry) (three)	dritte (<u>drî</u>-te) (third)
vier (veer) (four)	vierte (<u>feer</u>-te) (fourth)
fünf (fuunf) (five)	fünfte (<u>fuunf</u>-te) (fifth)
sechs (zêks) (six)	sechste (<u>zêks</u>-te) (sixth)
sieben (zeebn) (seven)	siebte (<u>zeeb</u>-te) (seventh)
acht (âHt) (eight)	achte (<u>âH</u>-te) (eighth)
neun (noyn) (nine)	neunte (<u>noyn</u>-te) (ninth)
zehn (tsehn) (ten)	zehnte (<u>tsehn</u>-te) (tenth)
siebzehn (<u>zeeb</u>-tsehn) (seventeen)	siebzehnte (<u>zeeb</u>-tsehn-te) (seventeenth)

You form the ordinal numbers above 19 by adding the suffix "ste" to the cardinal numbers. For example:

✔ **zwanzig** *(tsvân-tsîgk)* (twenty) / **zwanzigste** *(tsvân-tsîgks-te)* (twentieth)

✔ **dreissig** *(dry-sîgk)* (thirty) / **dreissigste** *(dry-sîgks-te)* (thirtieth)

✔ **vierzig** *(fîr-tsîgk)* (forty) / **vierzigste** *(fîr-tsîgks-te)* (fortieth)

Because ordinal numbers are adjectives, they take the gender and case of the noun they refer to. Table 3-2 shows you how the adjective **erste** *(êrs-te)* (first) changes in each case along with the article that comes before it.

Table 3-2	Declining Erste (êrs-te) (first)			
Noun's Gender	**Nominative**	**Genitive**	**Dative**	**Accusative**
Masculine (der)	der erste	des ersten	dem ersten	den ersten
Feminine (die)	die erste	der ersten	der ersten	die erste
Neuter (das)	das erste	des ersten	dem ersten	das erste
Plural (die)	die ersten	der ersten	den ersten	die ersten

Telling Time

To ask the time in German, you can use one of the following phrases:

✔ **Wie viel Uhr ist es?** *(vee feel oor îst ês)* (What time is it?)

✔ **Wie spät ist es?** *(vee shpeht îst ês)* (What time is it?)

German speakers can answer these questions in one of two ways: the "old-fashioned" way that uses the numbers on a standard clock (1 to 12), or by a 24-hour format, which we discuss in "Using the 24-hour routine: 0 to 24" later in this chapter.

Many German speakers use the 12-hour format when talking casually and revert to the 24-hour format when they want to make absolutely sure there's no room for misunderstandings, for example when discussing schedules.

Telling time the "old-fashioned" way: From 1 to 12

Telling the time at the top of the hour in the 12-hour system is very easy. You just say

Es ist . . . Uhr. *(ês îst . . . oor)* (It's . . . o'clock.)

substituting the number of the appropriate hour.

The following phrases show you how to use the German word for quarter (of course, you need to insert the appropriate hour in the phrases):

✔ **Es ist Viertel nach . . .** *(ês îst fîr-tl nâH . . .)*
(It's a quarter past . . .)

✔ **Es ist Viertel vor . . .** *(ês îst fîr-tl fohr . . .)*
(It's a quarter to . . .)

✔ **Es ist Dreiviertel. . .** *(ês îst dry-fîr-tl. . .)*
(It's a quarter to . . .)

When telling time on the half hour, German speakers always refer to it being a half hour before the next hour, rather than it being half an hour after the last hour. For example, in German, when it's 4:30, you say that it's half an hour before 5:00 rather than it being half an hour after 4:00. In German, to say 4:30, you say **Es ist halb fünf** *(ês îst hâlp fuunf)*.

Es ist halb . . . *(ês îst hâlp . . .)* (It's half an hour before . . .)

To express a time in terms of minutes before or after the hour:

> ✔ **Es ist fünf Minuten vor zwölf.** _(ês îst fuunf mî-noo-tn fohr tsvuolf)_ (It's five minutes to twelve.)
>
> ✔ **Es ist zwanzig Minuten nach sechs.** _(ês îst tsvân-tsîk mi-noo-tn nâH sêks)_ (It's twenty minutes past six.)

Leaving out the word **Minuten** in phrases such as those in the preceding list is common. Don't get confused if you hear someone say **Es ist fünf vor zwölf** instead of **Es ist fünf Minuten vor zwölf.**

Using the 24-hour routine: 0 to 24

With the 24-hour system, after you've reached 12, you keep on adding hours until you get to 24 or **Mitternacht** _(mî-ter-nâHt)_ (midnight), which is also referred to as **null Uhr** _(nûl oor)_ (literally: zero hour).

In this system of telling time, everything is expressed in terms of minutes after the hour. Note in the following examples how the hour comes first and then the minutes:

> ✔ **Es ist 15 Uhr dreißig.** _(ês îst fuunf-tsehn oor dry-sîgk)_ (It's 15 [hundred hours] and 30.) This corresponds to 3:30 p.m.
>
> ✔ **Es ist 21 Uhr fünfzehn.** _(ês îst ayn-ûn-tsvân-tzîgk oor fuunf-tsehn)_ (It's 21 [hundred hours] and 15.) That's 9:15 p.m. to you and me.
>
> ✔ **Es ist 22 Uhr vierundvierzig.** _(ês îst tsvy-ûn-tsvân-tsîgk oor feer-ûn-fîr-tsîgk)_ (It's 22 [hundred hours] and 44.) You got it — it's 10:44 p.m.
>
> ✔ **Es ist null Uhr siebenundreißig.** _(ês îst nûl oor zee-bn-ûn-dry-sîgk)_ (It's zero hours and 37.) Don't you think it's time to go to bed — it's 12:37 a.m!

Times of the day

This section details how the day gets divided up in German. Don't take the following time periods too literally, though; they're meant as a guideline. Just as in English, different speakers may have slightly different ideas about when one part of the day starts and another ends.

- ✔ **der Morgen** *(dehr môr-gn)* (morning; 4 a.m. to noon)
- ✔ **der Vormittag** *(dehr fohr-mî-tahgk)* (morning; 9 a.m. to noon)
- ✔ **der Mittag** *(dehr mî-tahgk)* (noon; 12 noon to 2 p.m.)
- ✔ **der Nachmittag** *(dehr nâH-mî-tahgk)* (afternoon; 2 p.m. to 6 p.m.)
- ✔ **der Abend** *(dehr ah-bnt)* (evening; 6 p.m. to 12 p.m.)
- ✔ **die Nacht** *(dee nâHt)* (night time; 12 p.m. to 4 a.m.)

Monday, Tuesday: Weekdays

The following days of **die Woche** *(dee wô-He)* (the week) are all the same gender, masculine **(der),** but generally they're used without an article. For example, if you want to say that today is Monday, you'd say **Heute ist Montag** *(hoy-te îst mohn-tahgk)*.

Without further ado, the days of the week are as follows:

- ✔ **Montag** *(mohn-tahgk)* (Monday)
- ✔ **Dienstag** *(deens-tahgk)* (Tuesday)
- ✔ **Mittwoch** *(mît-vôH)* (Wednesday)
- ✔ **Donnerstag** *(dônrs-tahgk)* (Thursday)
- ✔ **Freitag** *(fry-tâgk)* (Friday)

✔ **Samstag / Sonnabend** (*zâms-tahgk / zôn-ah-bênt*) (Saturday)

✔ **Sonntag** (*zôn-tahgk*) (Sunday)

Remember that the German week starts on Monday and not on Sunday.

The following forms indicate that something always happens on a particular day of the week. For example, you may get to a museum or a restaurant and find it closed. It may have a sign on the door reading **montags geschlossen** (*mohn-tahgks ge-shlôsn*) (closed on Mondays):

✔ **montags** (*mohn-tahgks*) (Mondays)

✔ **dienstags** (*deens-tahgks*) (Tuesdays)

✔ **mittwochs** (*mît-vôHs*) (Wednesdays)

✔ **donnerstags** (*dônrs-tahgks*) (Thursdays)

✔ **freitags** (*fry-tahgks*) (Fridays)

✔ **samstags / sonnabends** (*zâms-tahgks / zôn-ah-bênts*) (Saturdays)

✔ **sonntags** (*zôn-tahgks*) (Sundays)

If today is Monday, and you want to refer to an event that will happen on Tuesday, you don't say, "That's happening on Tuesday." Rather, you say, "That's happening tomorrow." Use the following words to help refer to specific days:

✔ **heute** (*hoy-te*) (today)

✔ **gestern** (*gês-tern*) (yesterday)

✔ **vorgestern** (*fohr-gês-tern*) (day before yesterday)

✔ **morgen** (*môr-gn*) (tomorrow)

✔ **übermorgen** (*uu-ber-môr-gn*) (day after tomorrow)

To speak precisely about a particular time on a specific day, you can combine the preceding words with the times of day. Try the following examples on for size:

✔ **heute Morgen** (*hoy-te môr-gn*) (this morning)

✔ **heute Vormittag** (*hoy-te vohr-mî-tahgk*) (this morning)

✔ **gestern Abend** (*gês-tern ah-bnt*) (yesterday evening / last night)

The word **morgen** (*môr-gn*) shows up in two different versions. Written with a lower case 'm,' **morgen** means tomorrow. The noun **der Morgen** written with upper case 'm' means morning. Theoretically, you could say, "morgen Morgen," to mean "tomorrow morning," but German speakers don't do that. Instead, they say **morgen früh** (*môr-gn fruu*).

Morgen, morgen does, however, exist. It's the beginning of a German proverb, and sometimes only the auspicious beginning is invoked. The complete proverb is

Morgen, morgen, nur nicht heute, sagen alle faulen Leute. (*môr-gn, môr-gn, nûr nîHt hoy-te zâ-gn â-le fow-len loy-te*) (Tomorrow, tomorrow, just not today, that's what all lazy folk say.)

Using the Calendar and Dates

September, April, June, and November may all have 30 days, but don't get overly confident yet — you still have to study the calendar.

Covering the units of the calendar

The following sentences show you how to build the calendar, **der Kalender** (*dehr kâ-lên-der*), in German:

✔ **Ein Jahr hat 12 Monate.** (*ayn yahr hât tsvuolf moh-nâ-te*) (A year has 12 months.)

✔ **Ein Monat hat 30 oder 31 Tage.** (*ayn moh-nât hât dry-sîgk oh-der ayn-ûnt-dry-sîgk tah-ge*) (A month has 30 or 31 days.)

✔ **Der Februar hat 28 oder 29 Tage.** *(dehr feh-brû-ahr hât âHt-ûn-tsvân-tsîgk oh-der noyn-ûn-tsvân-tsîgk tahge)* (February has 28 or 29 days.)

✔ **Eine Woche hat 7 Tage.** *(ay-ne vô-He hât zee-bn tah-ge)* (A week has seven days.)

The basic names of the months

The following list shows you all the names of the months. All the months' names are masculine, meaning that their article is **der:**

✔ **Januar** *(yâ-nû-ahr)* (January)

✔ **Februar** *(feh-brû-ahr)* (February)

✔ **März** *(mêrts)* (March)

✔ **April** *(ah-prîl)* (April)

✔ **Mai** *(my)* (May)

✔ **Juni** *(yoo-nee)* (June)

✔ **Juli** *(yoo-lee)* (July)

✔ **August** *(ow-gûst)* (August)

✔ **September** *(zêp-têm-ber)* (September)

✔ **Oktober** *(ôk-toh-ber)* (October)

✔ **November** *(nô-vêm-ber)* (November)

✔ **Dezember** *(deh-tsêm-ber)* (December)

Describing events in specific months

If something takes place in a particular month, you combine the name of the month with the preposition **im:**

✔ **Ich fliege im Januar ab.** *(îH flee-ge îm yâ-nû-ahr âp)* (I'm flying off in January.)

✔ **Ich fliege im Februar zurück.** *(îH flee-ge îm feh-brû-ahr tsû-ruuk)* (I'm flying back in February.)

✔ **Im März werde ich zu Hause sein.** *(îm mêrts vehr-de îH tsû how-ze zyn)* (In March, I'll be home.)

Naming specific times in the months

If you need to specify the time of the month, the following phrases help narrow down the field:

✔ **Anfang Januar** (*ān-fâng yâ-nû-ahr*) (in the beginning of January)

✔ **Mitte Februar** (*mî-te feh-brû-ahr*) (in the middle of February)

✔ **Ende März** (*ên-de mêrts*) (at the end of March)

Of course, you can substitute any month name after **Anfang, Mitte,** and **Ende:**

✔ **Anfang April fliegen wir nach Berlin.** (*ān-fâng â-prîl flee-gn veer nahh bêr-leen*) (In the beginning of April we'll fly to Berlin.)

✔ **Ich werde Ende Mai verreisen.** (*iH vêr-de ên-de my fêr-ry-zen*) (I'll go traveling at the end of May.)

✔ **Herr Behr wird Mitte Februar in Skiurlaub fahren.** (*hêr behr vîrt mî-te feh-brû-ahr în shee-ûr-lowp fah-ren*) (Mr. Behr will go on a skiing trip in the middle of February.)

Keeping track of dates

When talking about the date, **das Datum** (*dâs dah-tūm*), the day always comes first, and the month comes second (see Table 3-3). Note the period after the numeral identifying it as an ordinal number.

Table 3-3	German Dates, Long Version	
Write	*Say*	*Pronunciation*
1. Januar 2000	erster Januar Zweitausend	êrs-ter yâ-nû-ahr tsvy-tow-zênt
10. Juni 1999	zehnter Juni Neunzehnhundert- neunundneunzig	tsehn-ter yoo-nee noyn-tsehn-hûn-dêrt- noyn-ûnt-noyn-tsîgk

Write	Say	Pronunciation
20. März 1888	zwanzigster März Achtzehnhundert-achtundachtzig	<u>tsvân</u>-tsîgk-ster mêrts <u>âH</u>-tsehn-hûn-dêrt <u>âH</u>t-ûnt-<u>âH</u>-tsîgk

And now for the short version, which is popular for both the spoken and the written languages (see Table 3-4). The day still goes first, and the month goes second. Again, note the periods after the numerals (both the day and month are ordinals).

Table 3-4	German Dates, Short Version	
Write	**Say**	**Pronunciation**
1.1.2000	erster erster Zweitausend	<u>êrs</u>-ter <u>êrs</u>-ter tsvy-<u>tow</u>-zênt
2.4.1999	zweiter vierter Neunzehnhundert-neunundneunzig	<u>tsvy</u>-ter <u>feer</u>-ter <u>noyn</u>-tsehn-hûn-dêrt-<u>noyn</u>-ûnt-noyn-tsîgk
3.5.1617	dritter fünfter Sechzehnhundert-siebzehn	<u>drî</u>-ter <u>fuunf</u>-ter <u>sêH</u>-tsehn-hûn-dêrt-<u>zeep</u>-tsehn

If you want to find out what today's date is you ask:

Den Wievielten haben wir heute? *(dehn vee-feel-ten hah-ben veer hoy-te)* (What's today's date?)

The answer will be one of the following:

- ✔ **Heute haben wir den . . .** *(hoy-te hah-ben veer dehn)* (Today we have the . . .)
- ✔ **Heute ist der . . .** *(hoy-te îst dehr)* (Today is the . . .)

You may hear the name of a year integrated into a sentence in one of two ways. The first, longer way uses the preposition **im** to create the phrase **"im Jahr . . ."**, and the second, shorter way doesn't:

✔ **Im Jahr 2000 fährt Herr Diebold in die USA.** *(îm yahr tsvy-tow-zênt fehrt hêr dee-bôlt în dee oo-ês-ah)* (In the year 2000, Mr. Diebold is going to the United States.)

✔ **1999 war er in Kanada.** (noyn-tsehn-hûn-dêrt-noyn-ûnt-noyn-tsîgk vâr ehr în kâ-nâ-dâ) (In 1999 he was in Canada.)

Words to Know

das Datum	dâs dah-tûm	date
das Jahr	dâs yahr	year
der Kalender	dehr kâ-lên-der	calendar
der Monat	dehr moh-nât	month
der Tag	dehr tahk	day
das Vierteljahr	dâs fîr-têl-yahr	quarter
die Woche	dee vô-He	week

Money, Money, Money

In this section, we show you how to talk back about money. Whether you're speaking to a patient teller or an ultraefficient, impersonal ATM machine, a pocketful of the right expressions can get you . . . well, a pocketful of cash.

Changing currency

To talk about changing money, all you need are the
following phrases:

- ✔ **Ich möchte . . . Dollar in Euro einwechseln /
  tauschen.** *(îH muoH-te . . . dô-lâr în oy-ro ayn-vêk-
  seln / tow-shen)* (I would like to change . . . dol-
  lars into Euros.)

- ✔ **Wie ist der Wechselkurs?** *(vee îst dehr vêk-sel-
  kûrs)* (What's the exchange rate?)

- ✔ **Wie hoch sind die Gebühren?** *(vee hohH zînt
  dee ge-buu-ren)* (How high are the fees?)

- ✔ **Nehmen Sie Reiseschecks?** *(neh-men zee ry-ze-
  shêks)* (Do you take traveler's checks?)

When you exchange money, you may be
asked for your ID, so you need to have a
passport **(Reisepass)** *(ry-ze-pâs)* or some
other form of picture ID on you. The teller
will ask you

Können Sie sich ausweisen? *(kô-nen zee zîH
ows-vy-zn)* (Do you have proof of your ID?)

After you've proven that you are who you say you are,
the teller may ask you how you want the money:

Wie hätten Sie das Geld gern? *(vee hê-tn zee
dâs gêlt gêrn)* (How would you like the money?)

To which you can respond:

**In Zehnern / in Zwanzigern / in Fünfzigern / in
Hundertern, bitte.** *(in tseh-nern / in tsvân-zî-gern /
in fuunf-tsî-gern / in hûn-der-tern, bî-te)* (In bills of
10 / 20 / 50 / 100, please.)

Words to Know

der Ankauf	dehr __ân__-kowf	purchase / acquisition
sich ausweisen	zîH __ows__-vyzn	to show proof of identity
das Bargeld	dâs __bâr__-gêlt	cash
eine Gebühr bezahlen	__ay__-ne ge-__buur__ be-__tsah__-len	to pay a fee
Geld tauschen/ wechseln	gêlt __tow__-shen/ __vêk__-seln	exchange money
in bar	în bâr	in cash
Kasse	__kâ__-se	cash register
einen Reise-scheck einlösen	__ay__-nen __ry__-ze-shêk __ayn__-luo-zn	to redeem a traveler's check
der Schalter	dehr __shâl__-ter	teller window
der Verkauf	dehr __fêr__-kowf	sale
der Wechselkurs	dehr __vêk__-sel-kûrs	exchange rate
Wechselstube	__vêk__-sel-__stoo__-be	exchange bureau

Heading to the ATM

Instead of changing money at the teller window of a bank, you can also use an ATM machine, called a **Geldautomat** (_gêlt_-ow-tô-_maht_) in German. A typical run-through of prompts at the ATM may look like this:

- ✔ **Karte einführen** *(kâr-te ayn-fuu-ren)* (insert card)

- ✔ **Sprache wählen** *(shprah-He veh-len)* (choose a language)

- ✔ **Geheimzahl eingeben** *(ge-hym-tsahl ayn-geh-ben)* (enter PIN)

- ✔ **Betrag eingeben** *(be-trahgk ayn-geh-ben)* (enter amount)

- ✔ **Betrag bestätigen** *(be-trahgk be-shteh-tî-gen)* (confirm amount)

- ✔ **Karte entnehmen** *(kâr-te ênt-neh-men)* (remove card)

- ✔ **Geldbetrag entnehmen** *(gêlt-be-trahgk ênt-neh-men)* (take cash)

If you're unlucky, you may see the following messages:

Geldautomat außer Betrieb. *(gêlt-ow-tô-maht ow-ser be-treep)* (ATM out of service.)

Die Karte ist ungültig. / Die Karte ist nicht zugelassen. *(dee kâr-te îst ûn-guul-tîgk. / dee kâr-te îst nîHt tsû-ge-lâsn)* (The card is not valid.)

Die Karte wurde einbehalten. Bitte besuchen Sie uns am Schalter. *(dee kâr-te vûr-de ayn-be-hâltn. bî-te be-zoo-Hn zee ûns âm shâl-ter)* (The card was confiscated. Please see a teller.)

Chapter 4

Making New Friends and Enjoying Small Talk

. . . .

In This Chapter

▶ Introducing yourself

▶ Talking about your life

▶ Chatting up the family

▶ Shootin' the breeze about the weather

. . . .

*G*reetings and introductions are the first steps in establishing contact with other people and making an important first impression. Handled correctly, this first contact can open doors for you and help you meet people. If you botch your greetings and introductions, you may at best encounter a quizzical look — in the worst-case scenario, you may actually offend the person you're addressing! Read this chapter to make sure you don't embarrass yourself.

Hello! Greetings and Introductions

The following sections present plenty of simple German greetings that are essential for every beginning German speaker.

Saying hello and good-bye

The first part of your greeting is a basic hello. How you say hello depends upon what time of day it is. The most commonly used hellos include the following:

- ✔ **Guten Morgen!** *(gûtn môr-gn)* (Good morning!) Use this greeting in the morning (until about noon).

- ✔ **Guten Tag!** *(gûtn tahgk)* (Good day!) This greeting is the most common, except early in the morning and late in the day.

- ✔ **Guten Abend!** *(gûtn ah-bnt)* (Good evening!) Obviously, this greeting of choice is for in the evening.

- ✔ **Hallo!** *(hâ-lo)* (Hello!) Does this greeting sound familiar? It's basically the same in English.

When you need to take your leave, you can say

- ✔ **Auf Wiedersehen!** *(owf vee-der-zehn)* (Good-bye!) (formal):

- ✔ **Tschüß!** *(tshuuss)* (Bye!) (informal)

- ✔ **War nett, Sie kennenzulernen.** *(vahr nêt, zee kên-nen-tsû-lêr-nen)* (It was nice meeting you.)

- ✔ **Gute Nacht!** *(guh-te nâHt)* (Good night!) Use this greeting when you say goodbye late at night.

Asking "How are you?"

When you ask "How are you?", you either use the formal or the informal version of the question, depending on who you are talking to. You also have to remember to use the dative case of the personal pronouns **ich, du,** or **Sie.** (See Chapter 2 for more information on the dative case.)

Table 4-1 shows you how the dative case works.

Table 4-1	Personal Pronouns, Dative Case	
Pronoun	*Nominative Case*	*Dative Case*
I	ich	mir
you (informal)	du	dir
you (formal)	Sie	Ihnen

The formal version of "How are you?" is

Wie geht es Ihnen? *(vee geht êss ee-nen)*
(How are you? Literally, "How is it going?")

More informally, you use **dir:**

Wie geht es dir? *(vee geht êss deer)*
(How are you?)

If you really know someone well, you can go for the most casual version of the question:

Wie geht's? *(vee gehts)* (How's it going?)

Replying to "How are you?"

In English, the question "How are you?" is often just a way of saying hello, and no one expects you to answer. In German, however, people usually expect you to reply. The following are acceptable answers to the question "How are you?":

✔ **Danke, gut.** *(dâng-ke, gût)* / **Gut, danke.** *(gût, dâng-ke)* (Thanks, I'm fine. / Fine, thanks.) The literal translation would be "Thanks, good." / "Good, thanks."

✔ **Sehr gut.** *(zehr gût)* (Very good.)

✔ **Ganz gut.** *(gânts gût)* (Pretty good.)

✔ **Es geht.** *(êss geht)* (So, so.) The German expression actually means "it goes" and implies that it's not going too well.

✔ **Nicht so gut.** *(nîHt zoh gût)* (Not so good.)

As in English, the reply is usually accompanied by the question "And (how are) you?" which is an easy one. First the formal version:

> ✔ **Und Ihnen?** *(ûnt ee-nen)* (And you? formal)
>
> ✔ **Und dir?** *(ûnt deer)* (And you? informal)

Introducing yourself and others

Meeting and greeting often requires introductions. To introduce yourself, you can use one of the following two ways of telling people your name. One of them is

> **Mein Name ist . . .** *(myn nah-me îsst)* (My name is . . .)

There also is a verb that expresses the same idea, **heißen** *(hy-ssen),* which means "to be called":

> **Ich heiße . . .** *(îH hy-sse)* (My name is . . .)

To introduce someone else, all you need are the words

> **Das ist . . .** *(dâs îsst)* (This is . . .)

Then you simply add the name of the person. To indicate that you're introducing a friend, you say

> **Das ist meine Freundin** (f) / **mein Freund** (m) . . . *(dâs îsst my-ne froyn-dîn / myn froynt)* (This is my friend . . .)

If you're introduced to somebody in a slightly more formal setting, you can express "Nice to meet you" by saying

> **Freut mich.** *(froyt mîH)* (I'm pleased.)

The person you have been introduced to might then reply

> **Mich auch.** *(mîH owH)* (Me, too.)

If you're in a situation that calls for a very high level of formal introduction, here are some helpful phrases:

✔ **Darf ich Ihnen . . . vorstellen?** *(dârf iH* <u>*ee*</u>*-nen . . .* <u>*fohr*</u>*-shtêln)* (May I introduce you to . . .?)

✔ **Freut mich, Sie kennenzulernen.** *(froyt miH, zee* <u>*kên*</u>*-nen-tsû-*<u>*lêr*</u>*-nen)* (I'm pleased to meet you.)

✔ **Meinerseits.** (<u>*my*</u>*-ner-*<u>*zyts*</u>) / **Ganz meinerseits.** *(gânts* <u>*my*</u>*-ner-*<u>*zyts*</u>) (Likewise; literally, the pleasure is all mine.)

Following are a couple dialogs that involve introductions. First is one among younger people who meet in an informal setting, like a party:

Martin: **Hallo, wie heißt Du?** *(*<u>*hâ*</u>*-lo, vee hysst dû)* (Hello, what's your name?)

Susanne: **Ich heiße Susanne. Und Du?** *(iH hy-ssê zoo-*<u>*zâ*</u>*-ne. ûnt dû)* (My name is Susanne. And you?)

Martin: **Martin. Und wer ist das?** *(mâr-*<u>*tîn*</u>*. ûnt vear îsst dâss)* (Martin. And who is that?)

Susanne: **Das ist meine Freundin Anne.** *(dâss îsst* <u>*my*</u>*-ne* <u>*froyn*</u>*-dîn* <u>*ân*</u>*-ne)* (This is my friend Anne.)

Here is a dialog between two men, with one introducing his wife:

Herr Kramer: **Guten Abend, Herr Huber!** *(gûtn* <u>*ah*</u>*-bnt, hêr* <u>*hoo*</u>*-ber)* (Good evening, Mr. Huber!)

Herr Huber: **Guten Abend, Herr Kramer. Darf ich Ihnen meine Frau vorstellen?** *(gûtn* <u>*ah*</u>*-bnt, hêr* <u>*krah*</u>*-mer. dârf iH* <u>*ee*</u>*-nen* <u>*my*</u>*-nê frow* <u>*fohr*</u>*-shtêln)* (Good evening! Mr. Kramer. May I introduce you to my wife?)

Herr Kramer: **Guten Abend, Frau Huber! Freut mich sehr, Sie kennenzulernen.** *(gûtn* <u>*ah*</u>*-bnt frow* <u>*hoo*</u>*-bêr! froit mîH zehr zee* <u>*kên*</u>*-nen-tsû-*<u>*lêr*</u>*-nen)* (Good evening, Mrs. Huber! Very nice to meet you.)

Frau Huber: **Ganz meinerseits, Herr Kramer.** *(gânts* <u>*my*</u>*-ner-*<u>*zyts*</u>*, hêr* <u>*krah*</u>*-mer)* (Likewise, Mr. Kramer.)

Words to Know

auch	owH	also
freuen	froyn	to be glad / delighted
der Freund (m)	der froynt	friend
die Freundin (f)	dee <u>froyn</u>-dîn	friend
ganz	gânts	entirely, all
gehen	gehn	to go
gut	guht	good
kennenlernen	<u>kên</u>-nen-<u>lêr</u>-nen	to become acquainted with / to get to know
sehr	zehr	very
vorstellen	<u>fohr</u>-shtêln	to introduce

So Where Are You From?

In this section, you figure out how to tell people what city or country you are from and to ask them where they come from and what languages they speak. To do all this, you need to get familiar with a very useful verb: **sein** *(zyn)* (to be). You use this verb in the expressions **das ist** *(dâs îsst)* (this is) and **ich bin** *(îH bîn)* (I am). Unfortunately, it's irregular, so you just have to memorize it:

Conjugation	*Pronunciation*
ich bin	îH bîn
du bist (informal)	dû bîsst
Sie sind (formal)	zee zînt
er, sie, es ist	ehr, zee, êss îsst
wir sind	veer zînt
ihr seid (informal)	eer site
Sie sind (formal)	zee zînt
sie sind	zee zînt

Asking people where they come from

To ask somebody where they're from, you only need to decide if you're addressing somebody formally with **Sie,** or informally with **du** (one person) or **ihr** (several people). Then you choose one of these three questions to ask "Where are you from?":

✔ **Wo kommen Sie her?** *(voh kô-men zee hehr)*

✔ **Wo kommst du her?** *(voh kômst dû hehr)*

✔ **Wo kommt ihr her?** *(voh kômt eer hehr)*

To say where you're from in German, the magic words are

Ich komme aus . . . *(îH kô-me ows)*
(I come from . . .)

Ich bin aus . . . *(îH bîn ows)* (I am from . . .)

These few words go a long way. They work for countries, states, and cities. For example:

✔ **Ich komme aus Amerika.** *(îH kôm-me ows â-meh-ree-kâ)* (I come from America.)

✔ **Ich bin aus Pennsylvania.** *(îH bîn ows Pennsylvania)* (I am from Pennsylvania.)

✔ **Ich komme aus Zürich.** *(îH kô-me ows tsuu-rîH)* (I come from Zurich.)

- **Ich bin aus Wien.** *(îH bîn ows veen)* (I am from Vienna.)
- **Meine Freundin kommt aus Lyon.** *(my-ne froyn-dîn kômt ows lee-ôn)* (My friend comes from Lyons.)
- **Wir sind aus Frankreich.** *(veer zînt ows frângk-ryH)* (We are from France.)

Some countries' and regions' names are used with the feminine definite article, **die** *(dee)* (the). The United States is one such country. In German, you say **Ich bin aus den USA.** *(îH bîn ows dehn oo-êss-ah)* (I am from the U.S.). Or you might venture the tongue twister **Ich bin aus den Vereinigten Staaten.** *(îH bîn ows dehn fer-y-nîk-ten stah-ten)* (I am from the United States.).

Because the verb **kommen** *(kô-men)* (to come) is so important for discussing where you're from, here's the conjugation:

Conjugation	*Pronunciation*
ich komme	îH kô-me
du kommst (informal)	dû kômst
Sie kommen (formal)	zee kô-men
er, sie, es kommt	ehr, zee, êss kô-mt
wir kommen	veer kô-men
ihr kommt (informal)	eer kômt
Sie kommen (formal)	zee kô-men
sie kommen	zee kô-men

Understanding nationalities

Unlike English, where the adjective of a country's name is used to indicate nationality ("She is French"), German speakers like to indicate nationality with a noun. And as you already know, genders are important in German, and these nationality nouns have

genders, too. An American therefore is either
Amerikaner *(â-meh-ree-kah-ner)* if he is male, or
Amerikanerin *(â-meh-ree-kah-ne-rîn)* if she is female.

Table 4-2 lists the names of some selected countries,
plus the corresponding noun and adjective.

Table 4-2 Country Names, Nouns, and Adjectives

English	*German*	*Noun*	*Adjective*
Austria	Österreich (<u>uo</u>-ste-ryH)	Österreicher(in) (<u>uo</u>-ste-ry-Her[în])	österreich- isch (<u>uo</u>- ste-ry- Hîsh)
Belgium	Belgien (<u>bêl</u>-gee-ên)	Belgier(in) (<u>bêl</u>-gee-êr[în])	belgisch (<u>bêl</u>-gîsh)
England	England (<u>êng</u>-lânt)	Engländer(in) (<u>êng</u>-lain-der[în])	englisch (<u>êng</u>-lish)
France	Frankreich (<u>frânk</u>-ryH)	Franzose/ Französin (frân-<u>tsoh</u>-ze/ frân-<u>tsuo</u>-zîn)	französisch (frân-<u>tsuo</u>- zîsh)
Germany	Deutschland (<u>doytsh</u>-lânt)	Deutsche(r) (<u>doy</u>-tshe[r])	deutsch (doytsh)
Italy	Italien (î-<u>tah</u>- lee-ên)	Italiener(in) (î-tah-<u>ljeh</u>-ner[în])	italienisch (î-tah-<u>ljeh</u>- nish)
Switzerland	die Schweiz (dee shvyts)	Schweizer(in) (<u>shvy</u>-tser[în])	schweiz- erisch (<u>shvy</u>-tse- rîsh)
USA	die USA (dee oo-êss-<u>ah</u>)	Amerikaner(in) (â-meh-ree-<u>kah</u>- ner[în])	amerikanisch (â-meh-ree- <u>kan</u>-îsh)

The following examples show how to use these words
in sentences:

✔ **Frau Myers ist Amerikanerin.** *(frow myers îsst â-meh-ree-kah-ne-rîn)* (Ms. Myers is American.)

✔ **Michelle ist Französin.** *(mee-shêl îsst frân-tsuo-zîn)* (Michelle is French.)

✔ **Ich bin Schweizerin.** *(îH bîn shvy-tse-rîn)* (I am Swiss.)

✔ **Ich bin Österreicher.** *(îH bîn uo-ste-ry-Her)* (I am Austrian.)

What Languages Do You Speak?

To tell people what language you speak, you use the verb **sprechen** *(shprê-Hen)* (to speak) and combine it with the language's name (see Table 4-2 for a list of some common language names). But watch out: Although the adjective and the language for a country or nationality are identical, you capitalize the adjective when it's used on its own to describe the language:

Ich spreche Deutsch. *(îH shprê-He doytsh)* (I speak German.)

If you want to ask somebody if he or she speaks English, the question is

Sprichst du Englisch? *(shprîHst dû êng-lîsh)* (Do you speak English?) (informally)

Sprechen Sie Englisch? *(shprê-Hen zee êng-lîsh)* (Do you speak English?) (formally)

Here is the conjugation of the verb sprechen:

Conjugation	*Pronunciation*
ich spreche	îH shprê-He
du sprichst (informal)	dû shprîHst
Sie sprechen (formal)	zee shprê-Hen
er, sie, es spricht	ehr, zee, êss shprîHt
wir sprechen	veer shprê-Hen
ihr sprecht (informal)	eer shprêHt

Sie sprechen (formal)	zee <u>shprê</u>-Hen
sie sprechen	zee <u>shprê</u>-Hen

The following is a short conversation between two classmates using **sprechen:**

Heidi: **Sprichst du Französisch?** (*shprîHst dû frân-<u>tsuo</u>-zîsh*) (Do you speak French?)

Olga: **Nein, gar nicht. Aber ich spreche Englisch. Ihr auch?** (*nyn, gâr nîHt. <u>ah</u>-ber îH <u>shprê</u>-He <u>êng</u>-lîsh. eer owH*) (No, not at all, but I speak English. How about you?)

Heidi: **Ich spreche ein bisschen Englisch, und ich spreche auch Spanisch.** (*îH <u>shprê</u>-He ayn <u>bîss</u>-Hen <u>êng</u>-lish ûnt îH <u>shprê</u>-He owH <u>shpah</u>-nîsh*) (I speak a little English, and I speak Spanish, too.)

Olga: **Spanisch spreche ich nicht, aber ich spreche auch Englisch. Englisch ist einfach.** (*<u>shpah</u>-nîsh <u>shprê</u>-He îH nîHt, <u>ah</u>-ber îH <u>shprê</u>-He owH <u>êng</u>-lish. <u>êng</u>-lish îsst <u>ayn</u>-fâH*) (I don't speak Spanish, but I do speak English. English is easy.)

Words to Know

aber	<u>ah</u>-ber	but
ein bisschen	ayn <u>bîss</u>-Hen	a little
einfach	<u>ayn</u>-fâH	easy / simple
gar nicht	gâr nîHt	not at all
groß	grohss	large / big
interessant	în-te-re-<u>ssânt</u>	interesting
klein	klyn	small
nie	nee	never

continued

Words to Know (continued)

schön	shuon	pretty
sein	zyn	to be
sprechen	<u>shprê</u>-Hen	to speak
ich weiß nicht	îH wyss nîHt	I don't know

Talking about Yourself

What kind of job do you do? Are you studying? Where do you live? What's your address and phone number? These key questions are what you ask and answer when you talk about yourself.

Describing your work

What you do for a living often comes up in conversation. You may be asked one of the following questions:

- ✔ **Bei welcher Firma arbeiten Sie?** *(by <u>vêl</u>-Her <u>fîr</u>-mâ <u>âr</u>-by-tn zee)* (At what company are you working?)
- ✔ **Was machen Sie beruflich?** *(vâss <u>mâ</u>-Hen zee be-<u>roof</u>-lîH?)* (What kind of work do you do?)
- ✔ **Sind Sie berufstätig?** *(zînt zee be-<u>roofs</u>-teh-tîgk?)* (Are you employed?)

A couple of simple words and expressions help you answer these questions. Just connect **Ich bin** *(îH bîn)* (I am) with the name of your profession, without any article.

- ✔ **Ich bin Buchhalter** (m) / **Buchhalterin** (f). *(îH bîn <u>booH</u>-hâl-ter / <u>booH</u>-hâl-terîn)* (I am an accountant.)

✔ **Ich bin Student** (m) / **Studentin** (f). *(îH bîn shtû-dênt / shtû-dên-tîn)* (I am a student.)

If you're a student, you may want to communicate what you're studying. You do this with the phrase **Ich studiere** *(îH shtû-dee-re)* (I am studying). At the end of the sentence you supply the name of your field (without any article), which could include

✔ **Architektur** *(âr-Hî-têk-toor)* (architecture)

✔ **Betriebswirtschaft** *(be-treeps-vîrt-shâft)* (business)

✔ **Jura** *(yoo-rah)* (law)

✔ **Kunst** *(kûnst)* (art)

✔ **Literaturwissenschaft** *(lî-te-rah-toor-vîsn-shâft)* (literature)

✔ **Medizin** *(mê-dî-tseen)* (medicine)

Here are some other phrases to describe your employment status:

✔ **Ich bin pensioniert.** *(îH bîn pâng-zyô-neert)* (I am retired.)

✔ **Ich bin angestellt.** *(îH bîn ân-ge-shtêlt)* (I am employed.)

✔ **Ich bin geschäftlich unterwegs.** *(îH bîn ge-shêft-lîH ûn-ter-vehgks)* (I am traveling on business.)

✔ **Ich bin selbständig.** *(îH bîn zelpst-shtan-digk)* (I am self-employed.)

To tell someone where you work, use the phrase **Ich arbeite bei** *(îH âr-by-te by)* (I work at). In some cases, you may need to substitute another preposition for *bei.* For example:

✔ **Ich arbeite bei der Firma . . .** *(îH âr-by-te by der fîr-mâ)* (I work at the company . . .) After the word **Firma,** you simply insert the name of the company you work for.

✔ **Ich arbeite im Büro Steiner.** *(îH âr-by-te îm buu-roh shty-ner)* (I work at the office Steiner.)

Giving out your address and phone number

When someone asks you **Wo wohnen Sie?** *(voh voh-nen zee)* (Where do you live?), you can respond with any of the following:

- **Ich wohne in Berlin.** *(îH voh-ne în bêr-leen)* (I live in Berlin.) Just insert the name of the city you live in.

- **Ich wohne in der Stadt / auf dem Land.** *(îH voh-ne în dehr shtât / owf dehm lânt)* (I live in the city / in the country.)

- **Ich habe ein Haus / eine Wohnung.** *(îH hah-be ayn hows / ay-ne voh-nûng)* (I have a house / an apartment.)

Depending upon the circumstances, someone may ask you **Wie ist Ihre Adresse?** *(vee îst ee-re â-drê-se)* (What is your address?). To specify where you live, you need to know the following words:

- **die Adresse** *(dee â-drê-sse)* (address)

- **die Hausnummer** *(dee hows-nû-mer)* (house number)

- **die Straße** *(dee shtrah-se)* (street)

- **die Postleitzahl** *(dee pôst-lyt-tsahl)* (zip code)

When the time comes, you can substitute the appropriate word into the following sentence: **Die Adresse / Straße / Hausnummer / Postleitzahl ist . . .** *(dee â-drê-se / shtrah-se / hows-nû-mer/ pôst-lyt-tsahl îst . . .)* (The address / street / house number / zip code is . . .).

To tell someone your phone number, use this phrase:

Die Telefonnummer / die Vorwahl ist . . . *(dee tê-le-fohn-nû-mer / fohr-vahl îst . . .)* (The telephone number / area code is . . .).

Words to Know

dabei haben	dâ-by hah-ben	to have on/ with oneself
fragen	frah-gen	to ask
geben	geh-ben	to give
leider	ly-der	unfortunately

Talking about Your Family

Discussing families is a great way to get to know someone, and the subject gives you a wealth of topics when making small talk. You can find all the members of your family tree in the following list:

- **der Mann** *(dehr mân)* (man / husband)
- **die Frau** *(dee frow)* (woman / wife)
- **der Junge** *(dehr yûn-ge)* (boy)
- **das Mädchen** *(dâs mad-Hên)* (girl)
- **die Eltern** *(dee êl-tern)* (parents)
- **der Vater** *(dehr fah-ter)* (father)
- **die Mutter** *(dee mû-ter)* (mother)
- **die Kinder** *(dee kîn-der)* (children, kids)
- **der Sohn** *(dehr zohn)* (son)
- **die Tochter** *(dee tôH-ter)* (daughter)
- **die Geschwister** *(dee ge-shvîs-ter)* (siblings)
- **die Schwester** *(dee shvês-ter)* (sister)
- **der Bruder** *(dehr broo-der)* (brother)
- **der Großvater** *(dehr grohs-fah-ter)* (grandfather)
- **die Großmutter** *(dee grohs-mû-ter)* (grandmother)

- **der Onkel** *(dehr ông-kel)* (uncle)
- **die Tante** *(dee tân-te)* (aunt)
- **der Cousin** *(dehr koo-zeng)* (male cousin)
- **die Cousine** *(dee koo-zee-ne)* (female cousin)
- **die Schwiegereltern** *(dee shvee-ger-êl-tern)* (parents-in-law)
- **der Schwiegervater** *(dehr shvee-ger-fah-ter)* (father-in-law)
- **die Schwiegermutter** *(dee shvee-ger-mû-ter)* (mother-in-law)
- **der Schwiegersohn** *(dehr shvee-ger-zohn)* son-in-law
- **die Schwiegertochter** *(dee shvee-ger-tôH-ter)* daughter-in-law
- **der Schwager** *(dehr shvah-ger)* (brother-in-law)
- **die Schwägerin** *(dee shveh-ge-rîn)* (sister-in-law)

Saying that you have a certain type of relative involves the following simple phrase.

Ich habe einen / eine / ein . . . *(îH hah-be ay-nen / ay-ne / ayn)* (I have a . . .)

In this phrase, you're using the accusative (direct object case), so it involves different forms of the indefinite article for both gender and the case. The feminine and the neuter indefinite articles happen to be the same in the nominative (subject case) and accusative (direct object case). The masculine indefinite article, however, takes a different form in the accusative.

- **Masculine nouns:** Nouns like **der Mann, der Bruder,** and **der Schwager** use the form **einen.**
- **Feminine nouns:** Family members like **die Frau, die Tochter,** and **die Schwägerin** use **eine.**
- **Neuter nouns: Das Mädchen** uses **ein.**

If you want to express that you don't have siblings, you use the negative form of the indefinite article **ein** (*masculine*) / **eine** (*feminine*) / **ein** (*neuter*) (*ayn / ay-ne / ayn*) (a), which is **kein / keine / kein** (*kyn / ky-ne / kyn*) (no). The good news is that the negative form — **kein / keine / kein** — works exactly like **ein / eine / ein**. You just add the letter 'k.'

- ✔ **Masculine nouns,** such as **der Sohn: Ich habe keinen Sohn.** (*īH hah-be ky-nen zohn*) (I don't have a son.)

- ✔ **Feminine nouns,** such as **die Tochter: Ich habe keine Tochter.** (*īH hah-be ky-ne tôH-ter*) (I don't have a daughter.)

- ✔ **Neuter nouns,** such as **das Kind: Ich habe kein Kind.** (*īH hah-be kyn kīnt*) (I don't have a child.)

In the following dialog, two people talk about their families:

Michael: **Wohnen Sie in Frankfurt?** (*voh-nen zee īn fränk-fūrt*) (Do you live in Frankfurt?)

Lola: **Nicht direkt. Mein Mann und ich haben ein Haus in Mühlheim. Und Sie?** (*nīHt dee-rêkt. my-n mân ūnt īH hah-bn ayn hows īn muul-hym. ūnt zee*) (Not exactly, my husband and I have a house in Mühlheim. And you?)

Michael: **Wir haben eine Wohnung in der Innenstadt. Unser Sohn wohnt in München. Haben Sie Kinder?** (*veer hah-bn ay-ne voh-nūng īn dehr īn-nen-shtât. ūn-zer zohn vohnt īn muun-Hen. hah-bn zee kīn-der*) (We have an apartment in the center of the city. Our son lives in Munich. Do you have kids?)

Lola: **Ja, zwei. Mein Sohn arbeitet bei Siemens und meine Tochter studiert in Köln.** (*yah, tsvy. myn zohn âr-by-tet by zee-menss ūnt my-ne tôH-ter shtū-deert īn kuoln*) (Yes, two. My son works at Siemens, and my daughter is studying in Cologne.)

Michael: **Ach, meine Frau kommt aus Köln. Sie ist Juristin. Und was macht Ihr Mann beruflich?** *(âH, my-ne frow kômt ows kuoln. zee îsst yoo-rîs-tîn. ûnt vâss mâHt eer mân be-roof-lîH)* (Oh, my wife is from Cologne. She is a lawyer. What kind of work does your husband do?)

Lola: **Er ist Lehrer.** *(ehr îst leh-rer)* (He's a teacher.)

Talking about the Weather

People everywhere love to talk about **das Wetter** *(dâs vê-ter)* (the weather). Your good friend, the phrase **Es ist** *(ês îst)* (It is), helps you describe the weather, no matter what the forecast looks like. You just supply the appropriate adjective at the end of the sentence. For example:

- ✔ **Es ist kalt.** *(ês îst kâlt)* (It is cold.)
- ✔ **Es ist heiß.** *(ês îst hys)* (It is hot.)
- ✔ **Es ist schön.** *(ês îst shuon)* (It is beautiful.)

The following words allow you to describe almost any kind of weather:

- ✔ **bewölkt** *(be-vuolkt)* (cloudy)
- ✔ **feucht** *(foyHt)* (humid)
- ✔ **frostig** *(frôs-tigk)* (frosty)
- ✔ **kühl** *(kuuhl)* (cool)
- ✔ **neblig** *(neh-blîgk)* (foggy)
- ✔ **regnerisch** *(rehgk-ne-rîsh)* (rainy)
- ✔ **sonnig** *(sô-nîgk)* (sunny)
- ✔ **warm** *(vârm)* (warm)
- ✔ **windig** *(vîn-dîgk)* (windy)

Chapter 5

Enjoying a Drink and a Snack (or Meal!)

. . . .

In This Chapter
▶ Asking for your bread and butter
▶ Eating out
▶ Paying the check

. . . .

*F*inding out about the food and eating habits in another country is one of the most pleasant ways of discovering its culture. Business lunch or casual dinner, eating out or cooking for yourself — you just have to know your way around food.

"Enjoy your meal," or **Guten Appetit** *(gûtn âpe-teet),* as the Germans wish each other before they start to eat!

Is It Time to Eat Yet?

With the following phrases, you can voice when you're ready to eat or drink:

 ✔ **Ich habe Hunger / Durst.** *(îH hah-be hûngr / dûrst)* (I am hungry / thirsty.)

 ✔ **Ich bin hungrig / durstig.** *(îH bîn hûng-rigk / dûr-stigk)* (I am hungry / thirsty.)

To satisfy your hunger or thirst, you have to eat — **essen** *(êsn)* — and to drink — **trinken** *(trînkn).*

Essen is an irregular verb (see Chapter 2 for more information on irregular verbs):

Conjugation	Pronunciation
ich esse	îH ê-se
du isst	doo îst
Sie essen	zee êsn
er, sie, es isst	ehr, zee, ês îst
wir essen	veer êsn
ihr esst	eer êst
Sie essen	zee êsn
sie essen	zee êsn

And so is **trinken** *(trînkn)*:

Conjugation	Pronunciation
ich trinke	îH trîng-ke
du trinkst	doo trînkst
Sie trinken	zee trînkn
er, sie, es trinkt	ehr, zee, ês trînkt
wir trinken	veer trînkn
ihr trinkt	eer trînkt
Sie trinken	zee trînkn
sie trinken	zee trînkn

The three main **Mahlzeiten** *(mahl-tsy-ten)* (meals) of the day are the following:

- ✔ **das Frühstück** *(dâs fruuh-shtuuck)* (breakfast)
- ✔ **das Mittagessen** *(dâs mî-tahk-êsn)* (lunch)
- ✔ **das Abendessen** *(dâs ah-bnt-êsn)* (dinner)

You occasionally might hear people say **Mahlzeit!** *(mahl-tsy)* (literally, meal) as a greeting at lunchtime. If someone says this to you, just say the same — **Mahlzeit!** — back to them and smile. People commonly use this term in work environments (cafeterias and the office) to wish each other an undisturbed (and originally a blessed) meal time. You'll hear it any time between 11 a.m. and 2 p.m. anywhere in the workplace.

Setting the Table

The German table features all the same items that you find on your table at home, including the following:

- ✔ **das Besteck** (*dâs be-<u>shtêk</u>*) (a set of a knife, fork, and spoon)
- ✔ **die Gabel** (*dee <u>gah</u>-bl*) (fork)
- ✔ **das Glas** (*dâs glahs*) (glass)
- ✔ **der Löffel** (*dehr luoffl*) (spoon)
- ✔ **das Messer** (*dâs <u>mê</u>-ser*) (knife)
- ✔ **die Serviette** (*dee sêrv-<u>yet</u>-te*) (napkin)
- ✔ **der Suppenteller** (*dehr <u>zû</u>-pen-têl-ler*) (soup bowl)
- ✔ **die Tasse** (*dee <u>tâ</u>-se*) (cup)
- ✔ **der Teller** (*dehr <u>tê</u>-ler*) (plate)

If you're in a restaurant and need an item not found on the table (for example, a spoon, fork, or knife), call the waiter over by saying

Entschuldigen Sie bitte! Kann ich bitte einen Löffel / eine Gabel / ein Messer haben? (*ênt-<u>shûl</u>-dî-gen zee <u>bî</u>-te kân îH <u>bî</u>-te <u>ay</u>-nen luoffl / <u>ay</u>-ne <u>gah</u>-bl / ayn <u>mê</u>-ser <u>hah</u>-bn*) (Excuse me, please. Can I please have a spoon / a fork / a knife?)

Going Out to a Restaurant

Going out to a restaurant in Germany is very similar to the United States, except for the language, of course. The following sections walk you through every aspect of dining out in German.

Distinguishing places to eat

If you want a particular kind of eatery, it helps to
know what different kinds are available:

- ✔ **das Restaurant** *(dâs rês-toh-rong)* (restaurant):
  You find the same variety of restaurants in
  Germany as in the United States, ranging from
  simple to very fancy establishments with corresponding menus.

- ✔ **die Gaststätte** *(dee gâst-shta-te)* (local type of
  restaurant): This type of restaurant is simpler
  where you typically don't expect a fancy menu
  and may find local specialties.

- ✔ **das Gasthaus** *(dâs gâst-hows)* / **der Gasthof**
  (gâst-hohf) (inn): You usually find these in the
  country. They often offer home cooking, and the
  atmosphere may be rather folksy.

- ✔ **die Raststätte** *(dee râst-shta-te)* (roadside restaurant): You usually find them on highways and
  motorways with service-station facilities and
  sometimes lodging. (Called **der Rasthof** *[dehr
  râst-hohf]* in Austria.)

- ✔ **der Ratskeller** *(dehr rahts-kê-ler).* This one is
  tough to translate literally. These restaurants
  are named after an eatery in the cellar of the
  town hall **Rathaus** *(raht-hows)*. You often find
  them in historic buildings.

- ✔ **die Bierhalle** *(dee beer-hâ-le)* / **die Bierstube**
  (dee beer-shtoo-be) / **der Biergarten** *(dehr beer-
  gâr-ten)* / **das Bierzelt** *(dâs beer-tzelt)* (beer hall
  / beer garden): Besides beer served from huge
  barrels, you can also order hot dishes (usually a
  few dishes-of-the-day), salads, and pretzels. The
  best-known beer halls are in Munich, Bavaria,
  where the **Oktoberfest** *(ok-toh-bêr-fêst)* takes
  place in late September. The nearest equivalent
  may be an English pub or an American sports
  bar, although the atmosphere may be very
  different.

✔ **die Weinstube** *(dee vyn-shtoo-be)* (wine hall): A cozy restaurant, usually found in wine-producing areas, where you can sample wine with bar food and snacks.

✔ **die Kneipe** *(dee kny-pe)* (bar-restaurant): You can also find this type of bar-and-restaurant combination in the United States, and it's usually not very fancy. You can have a drink at the bar or sit down at a table and order bar food.

✔ **das Café** *(dâs kâ-feh)* (cafe): This may range from a coffee shop to a more upscale establishment. Vienna and its cafe tradition are famous.

✔ **der (Schnell)imbiss** *(dehr shnêl-îm-bîs)* (snack bar, fast-food restaurant): Here you can get different types of food and peculiarities for take-out.

Making reservations

When making a reservation, the following words and phrases come into play:

✔ **Ich möchte gern einen Tisch reservieren / bestellen.** *(îH muoH-te gêrn ay-nen tîsh reh-zêr-vee-ren / be-shtê-len)* (I would like to reserve a table.)

✔ **Haben Sie um . . . Uhr einen Tisch frei?** *(hah-bn zee ûm . . . oor ay-nen tîsh fry)* (Do you have a table free around . . . o'clock?)

✔ **Ich möchte gern einen Tisch für . . . Personen um . . . Uhr.** *(îH muoH-te gêrn ay-nen tîsh fuor . . . pêr-zoh-nen ûm. . . oor)* (I would like a table for . . . people at around . . . o'clock.)

To get more specific about when you want the reservation, you can add one of the following appropriate phrases:

✔ **heute Abend** *(hoy-te ah-bnt)* (tonight)

✔ **morgen Abend** *(môr-gn ah-bnt)* (tomorrow night)

- **heute Mittag** *(hoy-te mi-tahgk)* (noon today)
- **morgen Mittag** *(môr-gn mi-tahgk)* (noon tomorrow)

So you would say:

- **Ich möchte gern für heute Abend einen Tisch reservieren.** *(îH muoH-te gêrn fuur hoy-te ah-bnt ay-nen tîsh reh-zêr-vee-ren)* (I would like to reserve a table for tonight.)
- **Haben Sie morgen Mittag einen Tisch frei?** *(hah-bn zee môr-gn mi-tahgk ay-nen tîsh fry)* (Do you have a table free tomorrow for lunch / around noon?)

When making your reservation, the restaurant host may make some of the following statements or questions:

- **Für wie viele Personen?** *(fuor vee fee-le pêr-zoh-nen)* (For how many people?)
- **Tut mir leid, um acht Uhr ist alles ausgebucht. Sie können aber um acht Uhr dreißig einen Tisch haben.** *(toot meer lyt, ûm âHt oor îst â-lês ows-ge-booHt. zee kuon-bêr ûm âHt oor dry-sîk ay-nen tîsh hah-bn)* (I'm sorry. At 8:00 everything's booked. But you could have a table at 8:30.)
- **Und Ihr Name, bitte?** *(ûnt eer nah-me, bî-te)* (And your name, please?)
- **Geht in Ordnung, ich habe den Tisch für Sie reserviert.** *(geht în ôrt-nûngk, îH hah-be dehn tîsh fuur zee reh-zêr-veert)* (Okay, I have reserved the table for you.)
- **Es tut mir leid. Wir sind völlig ausgebucht.** *(ês toot meer lyt. veer zînt fuol-ligk ows-ge-booHt)* (I'm sorry. We are totally booked.)

If you show up at the restaurant without a reservation, expect to hear one of the following:

✔ **In . . . Minuten wird ein Tisch frei.** *(în . . . mî-noo-tn vîrt ayn tîsh fry)* (In . . . minutes a table will be free.)

✔ **Können Sie in . . . Minuten wiederkommen?** *(kuon-nen zee în . . . mî-noo-tn vee-dêr-kômn)* (Could you come back in . . . minutes?)

Arriving and being seated

After you arrive at a restaurant, you want to take your seat, **Platz nehmen** *(pláts neh-mn)*, and get your **Speisekarte** *(shpy-ze-kâr-tê)* (menu). A waiter, **der Kellner** *(dehr kêl-nêr)*, directs you to your table. The following dialog helps you get a good table:

Customer: **Guten Abend. Wir haben einen Tisch für zwei Personen bestellt.** *(gûtn ah-bnt. veer hah-bn ay-nen tîsh fuor ztweye pêr-zoh-nen be-shtêlt)* (Good evening. We reserved a table for two people.)

Host: **Bitte, nehmen Sie hier vorne Platz.** *(bî-te neh-mn zee heer fôr-ne pláts)* (Please take a seat over here.)

Customer: **Könnten wir vielleicht den Tisch dort drüben am Fenster haben?** *(kuon-tn veer fee-lyHt dehn tîsh dôrt druu-bn âm fên-stêr hah-bn)* (Could we perhaps have the table over there by the window?)

Host: **Aber sicher, kein Problem. Setzen Sie sich. Ich bringe Ihnen sofort die Speisekarte.** *(ah-ber zî-Her, kyn prô-blehm. zêtsn zee zîH. îH brînge ee-nen zô-fôrt dee shpy-ze-kâr-tê)* (But of course, no problem. Sit down. I'll bring you the menu right away.)

Words to Know

bringen	brîng-en	to bring
dort drüben	dôrt druu-bn	over there
hier vorne	heer fôr-ne	over here
In Ordnung!	în ôrt-nûngk	Okay!
Setzen Sie sich!	zêtsn zee zîH	Sit down!
Tut mir leid!	toot meer lyt	I'm sorry!
vielleicht	fee-lyHt	perhaps

Deciphering the menu

Now comes the fun part — deciding what you want to eat. Of course, what's on the menu depends entirely on what kind of eatery you're in.

Breakfast

The following items may be offered **zum Frühstuck** *(tsûm fruuh-shtuuck)* (for breakfast):

- ✔ **der Aufschnitt** *(dehr owf-shnît)* (cold meats and cheese)
- ✔ **das Brot** *(dâs broht)* (bread)
- ✔ **das Brötchen** *(dâs bruoht-Hên)* (roll)
- ✔ **die Butter** *(dee bû-têr)* (butter)
- ✔ **die Cerealien** *(dee tseh-rê-ah-lî-en)* (cereal)
- ✔ **das Ei** *(dâs ay)* (egg)
- ✔ **die Milch** *(dee mîlH)* (milk)
- ✔ **das Müsli** *(dâs muus-lee)* (muesli)
- ✔ **die Rühreier** *(dee ruuhr-ay-êr)* (scrambled eggs)
- ✔ **der Saft** *(dehr zâft)* (juice)

✔ **das Spiegelei** *(dâs shpee-gêl-ay)* (fried egg)

✔ **der Toast** *(dehr tohst)* (toast)

✔ **die Wurst** *(dee vûrst)* (sausage)

Appetizers

For **Vorspeisen** *(fohr-shpy-zen)* (appetizers), you may see the following:

✔ **Gemischter Salat** *(ge-mîsh-ter zâ-laht)* (mixed salad)

✔ **Grüner Salat** *(gruu-ner zâ-laht)* (green salad)

✔ **Melone mit Schinken** *(mê-loh-ne mît shing-ken)* (melon with ham)

✔ **Meeresfrüchtesalat mit Toastecken** *(meh-res-fruuH-te-zâ-laht mît tohst-êkn)* (seafood salad with toast halves)

Soups

You may see the following **Suppen** *(zû-pen)* (soups) on the menu:

✔ **Bohnensuppe** *(boh-nen-zû-pe)* (bean soup)

✔ **Französische Zwiebelsuppe** *(frân-tsuo-zî-she tsvee-bêl-zû-pe)* (French onion soup)

✔ **Ochsenschwanzsuppe** *(ok-sên-shvânts-zûp-pe)* (oxtail soup)

✔ **Tomatensuppe** *(tô-mah-tn-zû-pe)* (tomato soup)

Main dishes

Hauptspeisen *(howpt-shpy-zen)* (main dishes) are as diverse as they are in any culture:

✔ **Fisch des Tages** *(fîsh dês tah-ges)* (fish of the day)

✔ **Frischer Spargel mit Kalbsschnitzel oder Räucherschinken / Kochschinken** *(frî-sher shpâr-gel mît kâlbs-shnî-tsel oh-der roy-Her-shîng-ken / kôH-shîng-ken)* (fresh asparagus with veal cutlet or smoked ham / ham)

- ✔ **Hühnerfrikassee mit Butterreis** *(huu-ner-frî-kâ-seh mît bû-ter-rys)* (chicken fricassee with butter rice)

- ✔ **Kalbsleber mit Kartoffelpüree** *(kâlps-leh-ber mît kâr-tofl-puu-reh)* (veal liver with mashed potatoes)

- ✔ **Lachs an Safransoße mit Spinat und Salzkartoffeln** *(laks ân zâf-rahn-zoh-se mît shpî-naht ûnt zâlts-kâr-tofln)* (salmon in saffron sauce with spinach and salt potatoes)

- ✔ **Lammkotelett nach Art des Hauses** *(lâm-kôt-lêt nahH ahrt dês how-zes)* (homestyle lamb chop)

- ✔ **Rindersteak mit Pommes Frites und gemischtem Gemüse** *(rîn-der-steak mît pôm frît ûnt ge-mîsh-tem ge-muu-ze)* (beef steak with french fries and mixed vegetables)

Side dishes

You can sometimes order **Beilagen** *(by-lah-gen)* (side dishes) separately from your main course:

- ✔ **Bratkartoffeln** *(braht-kâr-tôfln)* (fried potatoes)

- ✔ **Butterbohnen** *(bû-ter-boh-nen)* (butter beans)

- ✔ **Gurkensalat** *(gûr-ken-zâ-laht)* (cucumber salad)

Dessert

German restaurants commonly offer many fine dishes **zum Nachtisch** *(ztuhm naH-tîsh)* (for dessert), including the following:

- ✔ **Apfelstrudel** *(âpfl-shtroo-del)* (apple strudel)

- ✔ **Frischer Obstsalat** *(frî-sher ohbst-zâ-laht)* (fresh fruit salad)

- ✔ **Gemischtes Eis mit Sahne** *(ge-mîsh-tes ays mît zah-ne)* (ice cream in different flavors with whipped cream)

- ✔ **Rote Grütze mit Vanillesoße** *(roh-te gruu-tse mît vâ-nîle-zoh-se)* (red berry compote with vanilla sauce)

Drinks

When ordering **Wasser** *(vâ-ser)* (water), you have the choice between carbonated or noncarbonated, which is **ein Wasser mit Kohlensäure** *(ayn vâ-ser mît koh-len-zoy-re)* (carbonated water) or **ein Wasser ohne Kohlensäure** *(ayn vâ-ser oh-ne koh-len-zoy-re)* or **ein stilles Wasser** *(ayn stîl-es vâ-ser)* (noncarbonated water). If you ask the server for **ein Mineralwasser** *(mî-nê-rahl-vâ-sêr)* (mineral water), you usually get carbonated water.

Wine is usually offered by the bottle — **die Flasche** *(dee flâ-she)* — or by the glass — **das Glas** *(dâs glahs)*. Sometimes, you can also get a carafe of wine, which is **die Karaffe** *(dee kah-râ-fe)*.

In the following list, you find a few common drinks, **Getränke** *(geh-traing-ke)* that you might see on a menu:

- ✔ **alkoholfreie Getränke** *(âl-ko-hohl-frye gê-tran-kê)* (nonalcoholic beverages)
- ✔ **Bier** *(beer)* (beer)
- ✔ **das Export** *(dâs ex-port)* / **das Kölsch** *(dâs kuolsh)* (less bitter, lager beer)
- ✔ **das Bier vom Fass** *(dâs beer fôm fâs)* (draft beer)
- ✔ **das Pils / Pilsener** *(dâs pîls / pîlze-ner)* (bitter, lager beer)
- ✔ **das Altbier** *(dâs âlt-beer)* (dark beer, similar to British ale)
- ✔ **Wein** *(vyn)* (wine)
- ✔ **der Weißwein** *(dehr vyss-vyn)* (white wine)
- ✔ **der Rotwein** *(dehr roht-vyn)* (red wine)
- ✔ **Champagner** *(shâm-pân-jer)* (sparkling wine made with French champagne method only)
- ✔ **Schaumwein** *(showm-vyn)* (sparkling wine, lower class)
- ✔ **Sekt** *(sêkt)* (sparkling wine, higher class)

✔ **der Tafelwein** *(dehr tah-fl-vyn)* (table wine, lowest quality)

✔ **der Kaffee** *(dehr kâ-fê)* (coffee)

✔ **der Tee** *(dehr teh)* (tea)

Placing your order

You can use the following expressions both for ordering anything from food to drinks and for buying food at a store:

✔ **Ich hätte gern . . .** *(îH ha-te gêrn)* (I would like to have . . .)

✔ **Für mich bitte . . .** *(fuor mîH bî-te)* (For me . . . please)

✔ **Ich möchte gern . . .** *(îH muoH-te gêrn)* (I would like to have . . .)

When ordering, you may decide to be adventurous and ask the waiter

Können Sie etwas empfehlen? *(kuon-nen zee êt-vâss êm-pfeh-len)* (Can you recommend something?)

You may need the following phrases to order something a little out-of-the-ordinary:

✔ **Haben Sie vegetarische Gerichte?** *(hah-bn zee veh-ge-tah-rî-she ge-rîH-te)* (Do you have vegetarian dishes?)

✔ **Ich kann nichts essen, was . . . enthält** *(îH kânn nîHts êsn, vâs . . . ênt-hailt)* (I can't eat anything that contains . . .)

✔ **Haben Sie Gerichte für Diabetiker?** *(hah-bn zee ge-rîH-te fuor deeâ-beh-tî-ker)* (Do you have dishes for diabetics?)

✔ **Haben Sie Kinderportionen?** *(hah-bn zee kîn-der-pôr-tseeo-nen)* (Do you have children's portions?)

Replying to "How did you like the food?"

After a meal, your server typically asks if you liked the food:

> **Hat es Ihnen geschmeckt?** *(hât ês ee-nen ge-shmêkt)* (Did you like the food?)

We hope you enjoyed your meal and feel compelled to answer that question with one of the following:

✔ **ausgezeichnet** *(ows-ge-tsyH-net)* (excellent)

✔ **danke, gut** *(dâng-ke, goot)* (thanks, good)

✔ **sehr gut** *(zehr goot)* (very good)

Getting the Check

At the end of your meal, your server may ask you the following to find out whether you're ready for the check:

> **Sonst noch etwas?** *(zônst nôH êt-vâs)* (Anything else?)

Unless you want to order something else, you need to pay **die Rechnung** *(rêH-nûngk)* (bill). You can ask for the bill in the following ways:

✔ **Ich möchte bezahlen.** *(îH muoH-te be-tsah-len)* (I would like to pay.)

✔ **Die Rechnung, bitte.** *(dee rêH-nûngk, bî-te)* (The check, please.)

You can pay together — **Alles zusammen, bitte.** *(â-les tsû-zâmn, bî-te)* (Everything together, please.) — or separately — **Wir möchten getrennt zahlen.** *(veer muoH-ten ge-trênt tsah-len)* (We would like to pay separately.).

If you need a **Quittung** *(kvî-tûngk)* (a receipt) for tax or other purposes, just ask your server after you asked for the check:

> **Und eine Quittung, bitte.** *(ûnt ay-ne kvî-tûngk bî-te)* (And a receipt, please.)

Words to Know

bezahlen	be-<u>tsah</u>-len	to pay
Bitte, bitte	<u>bî</u>-te, <u>bî</u>-te	You're welcome.
in bar bezahlen	în bâr be-<u>tsah</u>-len	to pay cash
die Kreditkarte	dee krê-<u>dît</u>-'kâr-te	credit card
die Quittung	dee <u>kvî</u>-tûngk	receipt
die Rechnung	dee <u>rêH</u>-nûngk	bill
Stimmt so!	shtîmt zoh	That's alright!

Like in most European countries, you don't need to tip your server unless the service was exceptionally good. The tip and tax is usually added in the final bill.

Chapter 6

Shop 'til You Drop

• •

In This Chapter

▶ Navigating stores

▶ Trying on and buying clothes

▶ Visiting the food markets

▶ Paying for your purchases

▶ Comparing apples and oranges

• •

*W*hether you're a hardcore shopper or just like window shopping — **Schaufensterbummel** (_shâû_-fêns-ter-_bû_-ml) — this chapter shows you the phrases you need to make your shopping experience a success.

Heading Out on the Town

When in Europe, you'll find myriad shopping opportunities in all kinds of venues, including the following:

  ✔ **die Boutique** (*dee boo-teek*) (a small, often elegant store generally selling clothes or gifts)

  ✔ **die Buchhandlung** (*dee booH-hând-lûng*) (bookstore)

  ✔ **das Fachgeschäft** (*dâs fâH-ge-shêft*) (specialty store)

  ✔ **der Flohmarkt** (*dehr floh-mârkt*) (flea market)

  ✔ **die Fußgängerzone** (*dee foos-gêng-er-tsoh-ne*) (pedestrian zone)

✔ **das Kaufhaus** *(dâs kowf-hows)* (department store)

✔ **der Kiosk** *(dehr kee-ôsk)* (news stand)

Getting around the store

When you decide to go shopping, you probably want to find out a store's hours. These questions can help:

✔ **Wann öffnen Sie?** *(vân uof-nen zee)* (When do you open?)

✔ **Wann schließen Sie?** *(vân shlee-sn zee)* (When do you close?)

✔ **Haben Sie mittags geöffnet?** *(hah-bn zee mî-tahgks ge-uof-net)* (Are you open during lunch?)

✔ **Um wie viel Uhr schließen Sie am Samstag?** *(ûm wee feel oor shlee-sn zee âm zâms-tahgk)* (At what time do you close on Saturdays?)

If you need help finding a certain item or section in a department store, you can consult the information desk — **die Auskunft** *(dee ows-kûnft)* or **die Information** *(dee în-fôr-mâ-tsyohn)*. They have all the answers, or at least some of them.

Shopping at night and on Sundays is still problematic in many places. Many stores close at 6 p.m. and don't open on Sundays, except certain specialty stores, such as some bakeries, and stores in big cities. The most likely place to find food or other necessities at night or on the weekend is still the **Tankstelle** *(tank-stêl-le)* (gas station).

If you're searching for a certain item, you can ask for it by name with either of these phrases (at the end of the phrase, just fill in the plural form of the item you're looking for):

✔ **Wo bekomme ich . . .?** *(voh be-kô-me îH)* (Where do I get . . .?)

✔ **Wo finde ich . . .?** *(voh fîn-de îH)* (Where do I find . . .?)

The people at the information desk can either say . . .
führen wir nicht *(. . . <u>fuu</u>-ren veer nîHt)* (We don't
carry . . .), or they can point you to the appropriate
section of the store, using one of the following
phrases:

- ✔ **Im Erdgeschoss.** *(îm <u>êrt</u>-ge-shôs)* (On the ground
  floor.)
- ✔ **Im Untergeschoss**. *(îm <u>ûn</u>-ter-ge-<u>shôs</u>)* (In the
  basement.)
- ✔ **In der . . . Etage.** *(în dêr . . . ê-<u>ta</u>-jhe)* (On the . . .
  floor.)
- ✔ **Im . . . Stock.** *(îm . . . shtôk)* (On the . . . floor.)
- ✔ **Eine Etage höher.** *(<u>ay</u>-ne ê-<u>tah</u>-jhe <u>huo</u>-her)*
  (One floor above.)
- ✔ **Eine Etage tiefer.** *(<u>ay</u>-ne ê-<u>tah</u>-jhe <u>tee</u>-fer)*
  (One floor below.)

If you want to browse through a section of the store,
you can use the phrase **Wo finde ich . . .?** *(voh
fîn-<u>de</u> îH)* (Where do I find . . .?), ending the phrase
with one of the following department or feature
names:

- ✔ **den Aufzug / den Fahrstuhl** *(dehn <u>owf</u>-tsûk /
  dehn <u>fâr</u>-shtool)* (elevator)
- ✔ **die Damenabteilung** *(dee <u>dah</u>-mên-âp-<u>ty</u>-lûng)*
  (ladies' department)
- ✔ **Haushaltsgeräte** *(<u>hows</u>-hâlts-ge-<u>ra</u>-te)* (domestic
  appliances)
- ✔ **die Herrenabteilung** *(dee hê-ren-âp-<u>ty</u>-lûng)*
  (men's department)
- ✔ **die Kinderabteilung** *(dee <u>kîn</u>-der-âp-<u>ty</u>-lûng)*
  (children's department)
- ✔ **die Rolltreppe** *(dee <u>rôl</u>-trê-pe)* (escalator)
- ✔ **die Schmuckabteilung** *(dee <u>shmûk</u>-âp-<u>ty</u>-lûng)*
  (jewelry department)
- ✔ **die Schuhabteilung** *(dee <u>shoo</u>-âp-<u>ty</u>-lûng)* (shoe
  department)

Browsing with style

Sometimes you just want to check out the merchandise on your own without anybody's assistance. However, store assistants may offer their help by saying something like the following:

- ✔ **Suchen Sie etwas Bestimmtes?** (<u>zoo</u>-Hen zee <u>êt</u>-vâs be-<u>shtîm</u>-tes) (Are you looking for something in particular?)

- ✔ **Kann ich Ihnen behilflich sein?** (kân îH <u>eeh</u>-nen be-<u>hîlf</u>-lîH zyn) (Can I help you?)

When all you want to do is browse, this phrase can help you politely turn down help:

Ich möchte mich nur umsehen. (îH <u>muoH</u>-te mîH noor <u>ûm</u>-zehn) (I just want to look around.)

The store clerk lets you know it's okay to keep browsing by saying either of the following:

- ✔ **Aber natürlich. Sagen Sie Bescheid, wenn Sie eine Frage haben.** (<u>ah</u>-ber nâ-<u>tuur</u>-lîH. <u>zah</u>-gn zee be-<u>shyt</u>, vên zee <u>ay</u>-ne <u>frah</u>-ge <u>hah</u>-bn) (Of course. Just let me know if you need help.)

- ✔ **Rufen Sie mich, wenn Sie eine Frage haben.** (<u>roo</u>-fn zee mîH, vên zee <u>ay</u>-ne <u>frah</u>-ge <u>hah</u>-bn) (Call me if you have a question.)

Getting assistance

In some situations, you may want or need some assistance. Here are some useful phrases you may say or hear:

- ✔ **Würden Sie mir bitte helfen? Ich suche . . .** (<u>vuur</u>-dn zee meer <u>bî</u>-te <u>hêl</u>-fn. îH <u>zoo</u>-He . . .) (Would you help me please? I'm looking for . . .)

- ✔ **Aber gern, hier entlang bitte.** (<u>ah</u>-ber gêrn, heer <u>ênt</u>-lâng <u>bî</u>-te) (But with pleasure. This way please.)

✔ **Welche Größe suchen Sie?** *(vêl-He gruo-se zoo-Hn zee)* (What size are you looking for?)

✔ **Welche Farbe soll es sein?** *(vêl-He fâr-be zôl ês zyn)* (What color do you want?)

✔ **Wie gefällt Ihnen diese Farbe?** *(vee ge-fêlt ee-nen dee-ze fâr-be)* (How do you like this color?)

Words to Know

die Abteilung	dee âb-ty-lûngk	department
der Aufzug	dehr owf-tsûgk	elevator
die Farbe	dee fâr-be	color
gefallen	gê-fâ-len	to like; to please
die Größe	dee gruo-se	size
hier entlang	heer ênt-lângk	this way
die Rolltreppe	dee rôl-trê-pe	escalator

Shopping politely

When asking somebody for help (or anything else, for that matter), it pays to add **bitte** *(bî-te)* (please) to your request. For example:

✔ **Wo finde ich Schuhe, bitte?** *(voh fîn-de îH shoo-e, bî-te)* (Where do I find shoes, please?)

✔ **Wo ist der Aufzug, bitte?** *(voh îst dehr owf-tsoogk, bî-te)* (Where is the elevator, please?)

When asking for help, you can be especially nice and say **Entschuldigen Sie, bitte . . .** *(ênt-shûl-dî-gen zee, bî-te)* (Excuse me, please . . .) at the beginning of your request.

✔ **Entschuldigen Sie, bitte, wo sind die Toiletten?**
(ênt-shūl-dī-gen zee, bī-te, voh zīnt dee tô-ah-lê-tn)
(Excuse me please, where are the bathrooms?)

✔ **Entschuldigen Sie, bitte, wo finde ich Winter-mäntel?** *(ênt-shūl-dī-gen zee, bī-te, voh fīn-de īH vīn-ter-mên-tel)* (Excuse me please, where do I find winter coats?)

If that phrase is too long for you, stick the word **Entschuldigung** *(ênt-shūl-dee-gūng)* (which actually translates as the noun "excuse") in front of whatever you're going to ask:

Entschuldigung. Wo ist der Ausgang, bitte?
(ênt-shūl-dee-gūng, voh īst dehr ows-gāng, bī-te)
(Excuse me, where is the exit, please?)

Shopping for Clothes

What is your heart's desire? Many terms for clothing are unisex, but some are usually reserved for one gender.

Some items usually meant for women include the following:

✔ **die Bluse** *(dee bloo-ze)* (blouse)

✔ **der Hosenanzug** *(dehr hoh-zn-ān-tsūgk)* (pant suit)

✔ **das Kleid** *(dās klyt)* (dress)

✔ **das Kostüm** *(dās kôs-tuum)* (suit)

✔ **der Rock** *(dehr rôk)* (skirt)

The following words usually apply to clothing for men:

✔ **der Anzug** *(dehr ān-tsoog)* (suit)

✔ **das Oberhemd** *(dās oh-ber-hêmt)* (button-down shirt)

The following items are generally considered to be worn by both men and women:

- ✔ **der Blazer** *(dehr bleh-zer)* (blazer)
- ✔ **das Hemd** *(dâss hêmt)* (shirt)
- ✔ **die Hose** *(dee hoh-ze)* (pants)
- ✔ **die Jacke** *(dee yâ-ke)* (cardigan, jacket)
- ✔ **das Jackett** *(dâss jhâ-kêt)* (jacket / sports coat)
- ✔ **die Krawatte** *(dee krâ-vâ-te)* (tie)
- ✔ **der Mantel** *(dehr mân-tl)* (coat)
- ✔ **der Pullover** *(dehr pû-loh-ver)* (sweater)
- ✔ **das T-Shirt** *(dâs t-shirt)* (T-shirt)
- ✔ **die Weste** *(dee vês-te)* (vest)

Of course, these items can come in any number of fabrics and styles, including the following:

- ✔ **die Baumwolle** *(dee bowm-vô-le)* (cotton)
- ✔ **das Leder** *(dâs leh-der)* (leather)
- ✔ **das Leinen** *(dâs ly-nen)* (linen)
- ✔ **die Seide** *(dee zy-de)* (silk)
- ✔ **die Wolle** *(dee vô-le)* (wool)
- ✔ **einfarbig** *(ayn-fâr-bîgk)* (solid color)
- ✔ **elegant** *(ê-le-gânt)* (elegant)
- ✔ **geblümt** *(ge-bluumt)* (with flowers)
- ✔ **gepunktet** *(ge-pûnk-tet)* (with dots)
- ✔ **gestreift** *(ge-shtryft)* (striped)
- ✔ **kariert** *(kâ-reert)* (checkered)
- ✔ **sportlich** *(shpôrt-lîH)* (sporty, casual)

Color me German

The basic **Farben** *(fâr-bn)* (colors) are

- ✔ **blau** *(blâû)* (blue)
- ✔ **gelb** *(gêlp)* (yellow)
- ✔ **grün** *(gruun)* (green)

- ✔ **lila** (<u>lee</u>-lah) (purple)
- ✔ **orange** (oh-<u>rongj</u>) (orange)
- ✔ **rot** *(roht)* (red)
- ✔ **schwarz** *(shvârts)* (black)
- ✔ **violet** (vee-oh-<u>lêt</u>) (violet, purple)
- ✔ **weiß** *(vyss)* (white)

Practice your clothes and colors using the following dialog between a store clerk and customer:

Clerk: **Kann ich Ihnen behilflich sein?** *(kân îH <u>ee</u>-nen be-<u>hîlf</u>-liH zyn)* (Can I help you?)

Customer: **Ja bitte. Ich suche eine Bluse.** *(yah <u>bî</u>-te. îH <u>zoo</u>-He <u>ay</u>-ne <u>bloo</u>-ze)* (Yes please. I'm looking for a blouse.)

Clerk: **Hier entlang, bitte. Welche Farbe soll es denn sein?** *(heer ênt-<u>lang</u> <u>bî</u>-te. <u>vêl</u>-He <u>fâr</u>-be zôl ês dên zyn)* (Please come this way. What color do you want?)

Customer: **Weiß.** *(vyss)* (White.)

Clerk: **Suchen Sie etwas Sportliches?** *(<u>zoo</u>-Hn zee <u>êt</u>-vâs <u>shpôrt</u>-lî-Hes)* (Are you looking for something casual?)

Customer: **Nein, eher etwas Elegantes.** *(nyn, <u>ê</u>-her <u>êt</u>-vâs eh-le-<u>gân</u>-tes)* (No, rather for something elegant.)

Clerk: **Gut. Welche Größe haben Sie?** *(goot, <u>vêl</u>-He <u>gruo</u>-se <u>hah</u>-bn zee)* (Good. What is your size?)

Customer: **Größe 38.** *(<u>gruo</u>-se <u>âH</u>-tûn-<u>dry</u>-sîgk)* (Size 38.)

Clerk: **Wie gefällt Ihnen dieses Modell?** *(vee ge-<u>fêlt</u> <u>ee</u>-nen <u>dee</u>-zes mô-<u>dêl</u>)* (How do you like this style?)

Trying it on

When you find something that looks promising, you may wish to try it on. You can ask the sales assistant the following question, supplying the name of the article that you want to try:

> **Kann ich . . . anprobieren?** *(kân îH . . . ân-prô-bee-ren)* (Can I try on . . .?)

A sales assistant may jump the gun and ask you

> **Möchten Sie . . . anprobieren?** *(muoH-ten zee . . . ân-prô-bee-ren)* (Would you like to try . . . on?)

In either case, you need to use the dressing rooms, which you can ask about by saying

> **Wo sind die Umkleidekabinen?** *(voh zînt dee ûm-kly-de-kâ-bee-nen)* (Where are the fitting rooms?)

After you try your item on, the sales assistant may ask you any of the following questions to find out if you liked what you saw in the dressing room:

- ✔ **Passt . . .?** *(pâst . . .)* (Does . . . fit?)
- ✔ **Wie passt Ihnen . . .?** *(wie past ee-nen . . .)* (How does . . . fit you?)
- ✔ **Gefällt Ihnen . . .?** *(ge-fêlt ee-nen . . .)* (Do you like . . .?)

You can answer with any of the following, depending on how everything went when you tried on your item:

- ✔ **Nein, . . . ist zu lang / kurz / eng / weit / groß / klein.** *(nyn, . . . îst tsû lâng / kûrts / êng / vyt / grohss / klyn)* (No, . . . is too long / short / tight / loose / big / small.)
- ✔ **Können Sie mir eine andere Größe bringen?** *(kuo-nen zee meer ay-ne ân-de-re gruo-se brîn-gn)* (Can you get me another size?)

✔ **... passt sehr gut.** *(... pâst zehr goot)* (... fits very well.)

✔ **... steht mir.** *(... shteht meer)* (... suits me.)

✔ **... gefällt mir.** *(... ge-fêlt meer)* (I like ...)

✔ **Ich nehme ...** *(ÎH neh-me ...)* (I'll take ...)

Take a look at these phrases in action:

✔ **Ich möchte die Bluse anprobieren. Wo sind die Umkleidekabinen, bitte?** *(îH muoH-te dee bloo-ze ân-prô-bee-ren. voh zînt dee ûm-kly-de-kâ-bee-nen, bî-te)* (I would like to try this blouse on. Where are the fitting rooms, please?)

✔ **Ja, natürlich. Hier entlang, bitte.** *(yah nâ-tuur-liH. heer ênt-lâng, bî-te)* (Of course. This way, please.)

✔ **Passt die Bluse?** *(pâst dee bloo-ze)* (Does the blouse fit?)

✔ **Ja. Ich nehme die Bluse!** *(jah. îH neh-me dee bloo-ze)* (Yes. I'll take the blouse.)

Words to Know

anprobieren	ân-prô-bee-ren	to try on
bringen	brîn-gn	to bring
eng	êng	tight
gefallen	ge-fâ-len	to like
... gefällt mir	ge-fêlt meer	I like ...
groß	grohs	big
kaufen	kow-fen	to buy
klein	klyn	small
kurz	kûrts	short

lang	lâng	long
das Modell	dâs mô-_dêl_	style
passen	_pâ_-sen	to fit
stehen	_steh_-en	to suit
die Umkleidekabine	dee _ûm_-kly-de-kâ-_bee_-ne	fitting room
weit	vyt	loose

Hitting the Markets

Sometimes you may not feel like eating out and may prefer to cook. You need to know where to go and what to buy.

The following is a list of stores where you might have to shop and the food groups they sell:

- ✔ **die Bäckerei** *(dee bai-ke-ry)* (bakery)
- ✔ **die Backwaren** *(dee _bâk_-vah-ren)* (bakery goods)
- ✔ **der Fisch** *(dehr fîsh)* (fish)
- ✔ **das Fleisch** *(dâs flysh)* (meat)
- ✔ **das Gebäck** *(dâs ge-_baik_)* (pastry)
- ✔ **das Gemüse** *(dâs ge-_muu_-ze)* (vegetables)
- ✔ **das Lebensmittelgeschäft** *(dâs _leh_-bents-mît-tel-ge-_shaift_)* (grocery store)
- ✔ **der Markt** *(dehr mârkt)* (market)
- ✔ **die Metzgerei** *(dee mêts-ge-_ry_)* (butcher shop)
- ✔ **das Obst** *(dâs ohpst)* (fruit)
- ✔ **die Spirituosen** *(dee shpî-rî-too-_oh_-zen)* (spirits)

✔ **der Supermarkt** *(dehr zoo-pêr-mârkt)* (supermarket)

✔ **die Weinhandlung** *(dee vyn-hând-lûng)* (wine store)

Finding what you need

In the various shops you may find the following wares. First, fruits and veggies:

✔ **der Apfel** *(dehr âpfl)* (apple)

✔ **die Banane** *(dee bâ-nah-ne)* (banana)

✔ **die Birne** *(dee bîr-ne)* (pear)

✔ **die Bohne** *(dee boh-ne)* (bean)

✔ **der Brokkoli** *(dehr broh-kôlee)* (broccoli)

✔ **die Erbse** *(dee êrp-se)* (pea)

✔ **die Erdbeere** *(dee ehrt-beh-re)* (strawberry)

✔ **die Gurke** *(dee gûr-ke)* (cucumber)

✔ **die Kartoffel** *(dee kâr-tof-fel)* (potato)

✔ **der Kohl** *(dehr kohl)* (cabbage)

✔ **der Kopfsalat** *(dehr kopf-zâ-laht)* (lettuce)

✔ **die Möhre** *(dee muoh-re)* (carrot)

✔ **die Orange** *(dee oh-rong-je)* (orange)

✔ **die Paprika** *(dee pâp-ree-kah)* (red, yellow, green bell pepper)

✔ **der Pilz** *(dehr pîlts)* (mushroom)

✔ **der Reis** *(dehr ryss)* (rice)

✔ **der Salat** *(dehr zâ-laht)* (salad)

✔ **das Sauerkraut** *(dâs zower-krowt)* (pickled cabbage)

✔ **der Spinat** *(dehr shpee-naht)* (spinach)

✔ **die Tomate** *(dee to-mah-te)* (tomato)

✔ **die Zucchini** *(dee tsu-kee-nî)* (zucchini)

✔ **die Zwiebel** *(dee tsvee-bel)* (onion)

If you're looking for some German fish and meat, brush up on the following:

- ✔ **die Bratwurst** *(dee braht-vûrst)* (fried sausage)
- ✔ **die Flunder** *(dee flûn-der)* (flounder)
- ✔ **das Hähnchen** *(dâs hain-Hen)* (chicken)
- ✔ **der Kabeljau** *(dehr kah-bel-yow)* (cod)
- ✔ **die Krabben** *(dee krâ-ben)* (shrimps)
- ✔ **der Krebs** *(dehr krehbs)* (crab)
- ✔ **die Muschel** *(dee mû-shel)* (mussel)
- ✔ **das Rindfleisch** *(dâs rînt-flysh)* (beef)
- ✔ **der Schinken** *(dehr shîng-ken)* (ham)
- ✔ **das Schweinefleisch** *(dâs shvy-ne-flysh)* (pork)
- ✔ **der Speck** *(dehr shpêk)* (bacon)
- ✔ **der Tunfisch** *(dehr toon-fîsh)* (tuna)
- ✔ **die Wurst** *(dee vûrst)* (sausage)

And don't forget your basic milk and bread:

- ✔ **das Brot** *(dâs broht)* (bread)
- ✔ **das Brötchen** *(dâs bruot-Hen)* (roll)
- ✔ **die Butter** *(dee bû-têr)* (butter)
- ✔ **der Käse** *(dehr kai-ze)* (cheese)
- ✔ **der Kuchen** *(dehr koo-Hen)* (cake)
- ✔ **die Milch** *(dee mîlH)* (milk)
- ✔ **die Sahne** *(dee zah-ne)* (cream)
- ✔ **das Schwarzbrot** *(dâs shvârts-broht)* (brown bread)
- ✔ **die Torte** *(dee tôr-te)* (tart)
- ✔ **das Weißbrot** *(dâs vyss-broht)* (white bread)

Asking for amounts

Asking someone in the open market or supermarket for something is just the same as ordering in a restaurant. You just say

Ich hätte gern . . . *(îH ha-te gêrn)* (I would like to have . . .)

At the end of that phrase, you get to tell the person what you want, which could include any of the following weights and measurements:

- ✔ **ein / zwei Kilo** *(ayn / tsvy kee-loh)* (one kilogram / two kilograms)
- ✔ **ein / zwei Pfund** *(ayn pfûnt)* (one pound / two pounds)
- ✔ **ein / einhundert Gramm** *(ayn / ayn-hûn-dêrt grâm)* (one / one hundred gram)
- ✔ **ein / zwei Stück** *(ayn / tsvy shtuuk)* (one piece / two pieces)
- ✔ **eine Scheibe / zwei Scheiben** *(ay-ne shy-be / tsvy shy-ben)* (one slice / two slices)

To specify exactly what you want, simply add the appropriate word to the end of the whole phrase. For example, if you want one kilo of apples, you would say

Ich hätte gern ein Kilo Äpfel. *(îH ha-te gêrn ayn kee-loh apfl)* (I would like to have one kilogram of apples.)

Words to Know

Das wär's.	dâs vêhrs	That's it.
das Gramm	dâs grâm	gram
das Kilo	dâs kee-loh	kilogram
das Pfund	dâs pfûnt	pound
Sonst noch etwas?	zônst nôH êt-vâs	Anything else?
wie viel	vee feel	how much

wie viele	vee <u>fee</u>-le	how many
Was darf es sein?	vâs dârf ês zyn	What would you like?

Paying the Bill

Once in a while, you may find yourself in a situation where you need to ask about the price **(der Preis)** *(dehr prys)* of something. The following simple phrases take care of the price question:

✔ **Was kostet . . .?** *(vâs <u>kôs</u>-tet)* (What does . . . cost?)

✔ **Wie viel kostet . . .?** *(vee feel <u>kôs</u>-tet)* (How much does . . . cost?)

When you're ready to make a purchase, refer to the following dialog between a clerk and customer for help:

Clerk: **Das macht 69.90 DM.** *(dâs mâHt <u>noyn</u>-ûnt-<u>zêH</u>-tsîgk mârk <u>noyn</u>-tsîgk)* (69.90 Marks, please.)

Customer: **Nehmen Sie Kreditkarten?** *(<u>nam</u>-en see kreh-<u>dît</u>-kâr-ten)* (Can I pay by credit card?)

Clerk: **Kein Problem.** *(kyn prô-<u>blehm</u>)* (No problem.)

Customer: **Hier bitte.** *(heer <u>bî</u>-te)* (Here, please.)

Clerk: **Danke. Würden Sie bitte unterschreiben? Und hier ist Ihre Quittung.** *(<u>dâng</u>-ke. <u>Wuur</u>-den zee <u>bî</u>-te unter-<u>schry</u>-ben? <u>ûnt</u> heer îst <u>ee</u>-re <u>qui</u>-toong)* (Thanks. Would you please sign here? And here is your receipt.)

Customer: **Danke!** *(<u>dâng</u>-ke)* (Thanks!)

Words to Know

kosten	kôs-ten	to cost
die Mehrwert-steuer (Mwst)	dee mêr-vêrt-shtoy-er	value added tax (vat)
der Preis	dehr prys	price

Chapter 7

Making Leisure a Top Priority

In This Chapter

▶ Going out on the town

▶ Heading to a party

▶ Talking about hobbies and sports

▶ Getting outdoors

*T*his chapter is all about having a good time — whether that means going out to a movie or a party or enjoying hobbies, sports, or the great outdoors.

Figuring Out What You Want to Do

Sometimes you want to go out by yourself, and sometimes you want company. If you want to brainstorm ideas with someone for the social calendar, you can ask:

Was wollen wir unternehmen? *(vâs vô-len veer ûn-ter-neh-men)* (What do we want to do?)

Use the following phrases if you want to find out about somebody's plans. These phrases are also very useful if you need to know if somebody is available:

> ✔ **Haben Sie (heute Abend) etwas vor?** *(hah-bn zee [hoy-te ah-bênt] êt-vâs fohr)* (Do you have anything planned [for tonight]?)

> ✔ **Hast du (morgen Vormittag) etwas vor?** *(hâst dû [môr-gn fohr-mî-tahgk] êt-vâs fohr)* (Do you have anything planned [for tomorrow morning]?)

> ✔ **Haben Sie (heute Abend) Zeit?** *(hah-bn zee [hoy-te ah-bênt] tsyt)* (Do you have time [tonight]?)

Going to the movies

When you want to go to the movies, use the following phrases to let everyone know:

> ✔ **Ich möchte ins Kino gehen.** *(îH muoH-te îns kee-nô gehn)* (I would like to go to the movies.)

> ✔ **Ich möchte einen Film sehen.** *(îH muoH-te ay-nen fîlm zehn)* (I would like to see a film.)

To get information about a movie:

> ✔ **In welchem Kino läuft . . .?** *(în vêl-Hêm kee-nô loyft . . .)* (In which movie theater is . . . showing?)

> ✔ **Um wie viel Uhr beginnt die Vorstellung?** *(ûm vee-feel oor be-gînt dee vohr-stê-lûng)* (At what time does the show start?)

> ✔ **Läuft der Film im Original oder ist er synchronisiert?** *(loyft dehr fîlm îm ô-rî-gî-nahl oh-der îst ehr zyn-krô-nee-zeert)* (Is the film shown in the original [language] or is it dubbed?)

> ✔ **Ich habe den Film gesehen.** *(îH hah-be dehn fîlm ge-zehn)* (I have seen the film.)

You can use the following phrases whenever you want to buy tickets, be it for the movies, the museum, the opera, or the theater:

> ✔ **Ich möchte . . . Karten für . . .** *(îH muoH-te . . . kârtn fuur . . .)* (I would like . . . tickets for . . .)

✔ **Die Vorstellung hat schon begonnen.** *(dee fohr-shtê-lûng hât shohn be-gô-nen)* (The show has already started.)

✔ **Die . . .-Uhr-Vorstellung ist leider ausverkauft.** *(dee . . .-oor-fohr-stê-lûng îsst ly-der ows-fêr-kowft)* (The show at . . . o'clock is unfortunately sold out.)

✔ **Wir haben noch Karten für die Vorstellung um . . . Uhr.** *(veer hah-bn nôH kâr-tn fuur dee fohr-shtê-lûng ûm . . . oor)* (There are tickets left for the show at . . . o'clock.)

✔ **Habt ihr Karten für die Matinee gekauft?** *(hâpt eer kâr-tn fuur dee mâ-tee-neh ge-kowft)* (Did you buy tickets for the matinee?)

Words to Know

die Eintrittskarte	dee ayn-trîts-kâr-te	ticket
die Karte	dee kâr-te	ticket
das Kino	dâs kee-nô	movie theater
laufen	low-fen	to show
der Platz	dehr plâts	seat
sehen	zeh-en	to see
der Spielfilm	dehr shpeel-fîlm	feature film
synchronisiert	zyn-krô-nee-zeert	dubbed
die Vorstellung	dee fohr-shtê-lûng	show

Going to the museum

Germany (as well as Austria and Switzerland) has a long and fruitful museum tradition with many venerable institutions sprinkled liberally across the country. If you want to go to one, just say

Ich möchte ins Museum gehen. *(îH muoH-te îns mû-zeh-ûm gehn)* (I would like to go to the museum.)

When you want to catch an exhibition — **Ausstellung** *(ows-shtê-lûng)* — some of the following phrases can come in handy:

✔ **Ich möchte die . . . Ausstellung sehen.** *(Ich muoH-te dee ows-shtê-lûng zehn)* (I would like to see the . . . exhibition.)

✔ **In welchem Museum läuft die . . . Ausstellung?** *(în vêl-Hem mû-zeh-ûm loyft dee . . . ows-shtê-lûng)* (At which museum is the . . . exhibit running?)

✔ **Ist das Museum sonntags geöffnet?** *(îsst dâs mû-zeh-ûm zôn-tahgks ge-ûof-net)* (Is the museum open on Sundays?)

✔ **Um wie viel Uhr öffnet das Museum?** *(ûm vee-feel oor uof-net dâs mû-zeh-ûm)* (At what time does the museum open?)

✔ **Haben Sie eine Sonderausstellung?** *(hah-bn zee ay-ne zôn-der-ows-shtê-lûng)* (Do you have a special exhibit?)

✔ **Wir wollen morgen um 10.00 Uhr in die Ausstellung.** *(veer vô-len môr-gn ûm tsehn oor în dee ows-shtê-lûng)* (We want to go to the exhibit tomorrow at ten o'clock.)

Bringing down the (opera) house

The following words and phrases may help you out on a trip to the opera or theater:

✔ **Ich möchte ins Theater / Konzert gehen.** *(îH muoH-te îns teh-ah-ter / Kôn-tsert geh-en)* (I would like to go to the theater / a concert.)

✔ **Ich möchte in die Oper gehen.** *(îH muoH-te în dee oh-per geh-en)* (I would like to go to the opera.)

✔ **Gehen wir ins Theater / Konzert.** *(gehn veer îns teh-ah-ter / kôn-tsert)* (Let's go to the theater / a concert.)

✔ **Gehen wir in die Oper.** *(gehn veer în dee oh-per)* (Let's go to the opera.)

✔ **Wann ist die Premiere von . . .?** *(vân îst dee prêm-yeh-re fôn . . .)* (When is the opening night of . . .?)

✔ **In welchem Theater spielt . . .?** *(în vêl-Hem teh-ah-ter shpeelt . . .)* (In which theater is . . . showing?)

✔ **Gibt es noch Orchesterplätze für die Matinee?** *(gîpt ês nôH ôr-kês-ter-plê-tse fuur dee mâ-tî-neh)* (Are there any orchestra seats left for the matinee?)

Words to Know

das Ballett	dâs bâ-lêt	ballet
der Beifall	dehr by-fâl	applause
die Kinokasse / Theaterkasse	dee kee-nô-kâ-sse / teh-ah-ter-kâ-sse	box office (movies) and theater
klatschen	klât-shen	to clap
die Oper	dee oh-per	opera / opera house

continued

Words to Know *(continued)*

die Pause	dee <u>pow</u>-ze	intermission
der Platz	dehr plâts	seat
der Sänger / die Sängerin	dehr <u>zên</u>-ger / dee <u>zên</u>-ge-rîn	singer
der Schau-spieler / die Schau-spielerin	dehr <u>show</u>-shpee-ler / dee <u>show</u>-spee-le-rîn	actor/ actress
singen	<u>zîn</u>-gen	to sing
tanzen	<u>tân</u>-tsen	to dance
der Tänzer / die Tänzerin	dehr <u>tên</u>-tser / dee <u>tên</u>-tse-rîn	dancer
das Theater	dâs teh-<u>ah</u>-ter	theater
die Zugabe	dee <u>tsoo</u>-gah-be	encore

How Was the Show? Talking about Entertainment

When it comes to entertainment, everybody seems to have an opinion. You don't want to miss out on the fun, do you?

The following two questions start you out (the first version is for speaking with someone formally; the second is for informal speaking):

✔ **Hat Ihnen die Ausstellung / der Film / die Oper gefallen?** *(hât ee-nen dee ows-shtê-lûng / dehr film / dee oh-per ge-fâ-len)* (Did you like the exhibition / the movie / the opera?)

✔ **Hat dir die Ausstellung / der Film / die Oper gefallen?** *(hât deer dee ows-shtê-lûng / dehr film / dee oh-per ge-fâ-len)* (Did you like the exhibition / the movie / the opera?)

To answer, try one of the following on for size:

✔ **Die Ausstellung / der Film / die Oper hat mir (sehr) gut gefallen.** *(dee ows-shtê-lûng / dehr film / dee oh-per hât meer zehr goot ge-fâ-len)* (I liked the exhibition / the movie / the opera [a lot].)

✔ **Die Ausstellung / der Film / die Oper hat mir (gar) nicht gefallen.** *(dee ows-shtê-lûng / dehr film / dee oh-per hât meer (gâr) nîHt ge-fâ-len)* (I didn't like the exhibition / the movie / the opera [at all].)

You may want to follow up that statement with a reason. Start out by saying:

Die Ausstellung / Der Film / Die Oper war wirklich . . . *(dee ows-shtê-lûng / dehr film / dee oh-per vahr vîrk-lîH . . .)* (The exhibition / the movie / the opera was really . . .)

Finish the thought with any of the following adjectives that may apply. (You can always string a few of these adjectives together with the conjunction **und** *[ûnt]* [and] if you like):

✔ **aufregend** *(owf-reh-gent)* (exciting)

✔ **ausgezeichnet** *(ows-ge-tsyH-net)* (excellent)

✔ **enttäuschend** *(ênt-toy-shênt)* (disappointing)

✔ **langweilig** *(lâng-vy-lîg)* (boring)

✔ **phantastisch** *(fân-tâs-tîsh)* (fantastic)

✔ **sehenswert** (<u>zeh</u>-êns-vehrt) (worth seeing)

✔ **spannend** (<u>shpâ</u>-nênt) (suspenseful)

✔ **unterhaltsam** (ûn-ter-<u>hâlt</u>-zahm) (entertaining)

✔ **wunderschön** (vûn-der-<u>shuon</u>) (beautiful)

Check out the following dialog for an example of an entertainment conversation:

Claudia: **Sind Sie nicht gestern im Theater gewesen?** (zînt zee nîHt <u>gês</u>-tern îm theh-<u>ah</u>-ter ge-<u>weh</u>-zen) (Weren't you at the theater last night?)

Ian: **Ich habe das neue Ballet gesehen.** (îH <u>hah</u>-be dâs <u>noy</u>-e bâ-<u>lêt</u> ge-<u>zehn</u>) (I saw the new ballet.)

Claudia: **Wie hat es Ihnen gefallen?** (vee hât ês <u>ee</u>-nen ge-<u>fâ</u>-len) (How did you like it?)

Ian: **Die Tänzer sind phantastisch. Die Vorstellung hat mir ausgezeichnet gefallen.** (dee <u>tên</u>-tser zînt fân-<u>tâs</u>-tîsh. dee <u>vôr</u>-shtê-lûng hât meer ows-ge-<u>tsyH</u>-net ge-<u>fâ</u>-len) (The dancers are fabulous. I liked the performance very much.)

Claudia: **War es einfach, Karten zu bekommen?** (vahr ês <u>ayn</u>-fâH, <u>kâr</u>-tn tsû be-<u>kô</u>-men) (Was it easy to get tickets?)

Ian: **Ja. Ich habe die Karte gestern Morgen an der Theaterkasse gekauft.** (yah, îH <u>hah</u>-be dee <u>kâr</u>-te <u>gês</u>-têrn môrgn ân dehr teh-<u>ah</u>-ter-<u>kâ</u>-se ge-<u>kowft</u>) (Yes, I bought the ticket at the box office yesterday morning.)

Going to a Party

If you're invited to a party, you may hear someone say, "It's my party, and I'll cry if I want to," but you don't want to be a party pooper, so use the following common phrases and have fun:

✔ **Ich würde Sie gern zu einer Party einladen.** (îH <u>vuur</u>-de zee gêrn tsû <u>ay</u>-ner <u>pâr</u>-tee <u>ayn</u>-lah-den) (I would like to invite you to a party.)

✔ **Wir wollen eine Party feiern. Hast du Lust zu kommen?** *(veer vô-len ay-ne pâr-tee fy-ern. hâst dû lûst tsû kô-men)* (We want to have a party. Do you feel like coming?)

To ask when and where the party is going to take place:

✔ **Wann findet die Party statt?** *(vân fin-det dee pâr-tee shtât)* (When does the party take place?)

✔ **Wo findet die Party statt?** *(vô fin-det dee pâr-tee shtât)* (Where does the party take place?)

If you can't make it (or don't want to go for some reason), you can politely turn down the invitation by saying the following:

✔ **Nein, tut mir leid, ich kann leider nicht kommen.** *(nyn, tût meer lyt, îH kân ly-der nîHt kô-men)* (No, sorry. Unfortunately, I won't be able to make it.)

✔ **Nein, da kann ich leider nicht. Ich habe schon etwas anderes vor.** *(nyn, dâ kân îH ly-der nîHt. îH hah-be shohn êt-vâs ân-de-res fohr)* (No, unfortunately, I won't be able to make it. I have other plans.)

If the time, place, and your mood are right, you can accept an invitation with the following phrases:

✔ **Vielen Dank. Ich nehme die Einladung gern an.** *(fee-len dângk. îH neh-me dee ayn-lah-dûng gêrn ân)* (Thank you very much. I'll gladly accept the invitation.)

✔ **Gut, ich komme gern. Soll ich etwas mitbringen?** *(goot, îH kô-me gêrn. zôl îH êt-vâs mît-brîn-gen)* (Good, I'd like to come. Would you like me to bring anything?)

To the question of whether you can bring something with you, your host may respond:

✔ **Nicht nötig. Für Essen und Trinken ist gesorgt.** *(nîHt nuo-tîg. fuur êsn ûnt trîn-ken îst ge-zôrgt)* (Not necessary. Food and drink are taken care of.)

✔ **Es wäre schön, wenn Sie . . . mitbringen.** *(ês vê-re shuon, vên zee . . . mît-brîn-gen)* (It would be nice if you brought . . . along.)

✔ **Es wäre schön, wenn du . . . mitbringst.** *(ês vê-re shuon, vên dû . . . mît-brîn-gst)* (It would be nice if you brought . . . along.)

Talking about Hobbies and Interests

Many people fill their leisure time with hobbies. This section shows you how to talk about yours. If you're a collector, you can tell people about your particular area of interest by saying either of the following:

✔ **Ich sammele . . .** *(îH zâm-le . . .)* (I collect . . .)

✔ **Ich interessiere mich für . . .** *(îH în-te-re-see-re mîH fuur . . .)* (I'm interested in . . .)

At the end of these phrases, you name the thing you like to collect. For example, you could finish with any of the following:

✔ **antikes Glas und Porzellan** *(ân-tee-kes glahs ûnt pôr-tse-lahn)* (antique glass and porcelain)

✔ **Antiquitäten und Trödel** *(ân-tî-kvî-teh-ten ûnt truo-dl)* (antiques and bric-a-brac)

✔ **Briefmarken** *(breef-mâr-ken)* (stamps)

✔ **Münzen und Medaillen** *(muun-tsen ûnt mê-dâl-yen)* (coins and medals)

✔ **Puppen** *(pû-pen)* (dolls)

Some people enjoy making things with their hands. Just use this simple phrase to introduce the topic:

Mein Hobby ist . . . *(myn h̲ô̲-bee îst . . .)* (My hobby is . . .)

At the end of this phrase, you supply the necessary information. For example:

- ✔ **Basteln** *(b̲âs̲-teln)* (crafts)
- ✔ **Gärtnerei** *(gêrt-ne-r̲y̲)* (gardening)
- ✔ **Kochen** *(k̲ô̲-Hen)* (cooking)
- ✔ **Malen** *(m̲ah̲-len)* (painting)
- ✔ **. . . sammeln** *(. . . z̲â̲-meln)* (collecting . . .)

Playing Sports

With the words and phrases we show you in this section, you'll be able to share your interest in sports with other people.

You can express your interest in playing many sports by using the verb **spielen** *(shpee-len)* (to play) in the following phrase:

Ich spiele gern . . . *(îH shpee̲-le gêrn . . .)* (I like to play . . .)

Insert the names of the following sports at the end of the sentence:

- ✔ **Basketball** *(b̲ahs̲-ket-bâl)* (basketball)
- ✔ **Fußball** *(f̲oos̲-bâl)* (soccer)
- ✔ **Golf** *(gôlf)* (golf)
- ✔ **Handball** *(h̲ânt̲-bâl)* (handball)
- ✔ **Tennis** *(t̲ê̲-nîs)* (tennis)

Some sports have their own verb. For them, you use the following expression to communicate what sport you're in the mood for:

Ich möchte gern . . . *(îH m̲uoH̲-te gêrn . . .)* (I would like to . . .)

Now just insert the appropriate sport verb at the end of the sentence:

- ✔ **Fahrrad fahren** *(fah-rât fah-ren)* (bike riding)
- ✔ **joggen** *(jô-gen)* (jogging)
- ✔ **schwimmen** *(shvî-men)* (swimming)
- ✔ **segeln** *(zeh-geln)* (sailing)
- ✔ **Ski laufen** *(shee low-fen)* (skiing)
- ✔ **Wind surfen** *(vînt surfen)* (wind surfing)

If you're just talking in general about a sport you like, use this phrase:

Ich . . . gern. *(îH . . . gêrn)* (I like to . . .)

Here you need to remember to conjugate the verb you fill in the blank. Check it out:

- ✔ **Ich schwimme gern.** *(îH shvî-me gêrn)* (I like swimming.)
- ✔ **Ich fahre gern Fahrrad.** *(îH fah-re gêrn fah-rât)* (I like bicycling.)

If you want to ask someone to join you in an activity, use one of the following expressions:

- ✔ **Lass uns . . . gehen!** *(lâs ûns . . . geh-en)* (Let's go . . .!)
- ✔ **Spielst du . . .?** *(shpeelst dû . . .)* (Do you play . . .?)

Words to Know

gewinnen	gê-vî-nen	to win
die Mannschaft	dee mân-shâft	team
das Spiel	dâs shpeel	game

| sich verletzen | zîH fêr-lê-tsen | to get hurt |
| tut mir leid | toot meer lyt | I'm sorry |

Exploring the Outdoors

Did you have a hectic week at work? Are you tired of waiting for your turn in the shower after the soccer match? Maybe you just want to get away from it all and experience the great outdoors alone or with your family and friends.

Getting out and going

When it comes to walking and hiking, the following phrases can get you on your way:

> ✔ **Wollen wir spazieren / wandern gehen?** *(vô-len veer shpâ-tsee-ren / vân-dêrn gehn)* (Should we take a walk?)

> ✔ **Ich möchte spazieren / wandern gehen.** *(îH muoH-te shpâ-tsee-ren / vân-dern gehn)* (I would like to take a walk / go hiking.)

Things to see along the way

When you return from your tour of the great outdoors, you can tell people about what you saw:

> ✔ **Ich habe . . . gesehen.** *(îH hah-be . . . gê-zehn)* (I saw . . .)

> ✔ **Ich habe . . . beobachtet.** *(îH hah-be . . . bê-ohp-âH-tet)* (I was watching . . .)

Just fill in the blanks. You may encounter any of the following on your tour:

- ✔ **der Baum** *(dehr bowm)* (tree)
- ✔ **der Fluss** *(dehr flûss)* (river)
- ✔ **das Gebirge** *(dâs ge-<u>bîr</u>-ge)* (mountains)
- ✔ **die Kuh** *(dee koo)* (cow)
- ✔ **das Meer** *(dâs mehr)* (sea, ocean)
- ✔ **das Pferd** *(dâs pfêrt)* (horse)
- ✔ **das Reh** *(dâs reh)* (deer)
- ✔ **das Schaf** *(dâs shaaf)* (sheep)
- ✔ **der See** *(dehr zeh)* (lake)
- ✔ **der Vogel** *(dehr <u>foh</u>-gl)* (bird)

Remember to use the accusative case when complet-
ing these sentences. (See Chapter 2 for more information on the accusative case.)

- ✔ For masculine nouns: **Ich habe einen Vogel
  gesehen.** *(îH <u>hah</u>-be <u>ay</u>-nen <u>foh</u>-gl ge-<u>zehn</u>)* (I saw
  a bird.)
- ✔ For feminine nouns: **Ich habe eine Kuh gese-
  hen.** *(îH <u>hah</u>-be <u>ay</u>-ne koo ge-<u>zehn</u>)* (I saw a cow.)
- ✔ For neuter nouns: **Ich habe ein Reh gesehen.**
  (îH <u>hah</u>-be <u>ay</u>n reh ge-<u>zehn</u>) (I saw a deer.)
- ✔ Or you may want to use plural, which is gener-
  ally easier: **Ich habe Vögel gesehen.** *(îH <u>hah</u>-be
  <u>fuo</u>-gl ge-<u>zehn</u>)* (I saw birds.)

Going to the mountains

Whether it's the ever-popular Alps or one of the other
mountain ranges that you're planning to visit, you're
sure to meet the locals. And before you join them, for-
tify yourself with some sustaining vocabulary:

- ✔ **Wir fahren in die Berge.** *(veer <u>fah</u>-ren în dee
  <u>bêr</u>-ge)* (We are going to the mountains.)
- ✔ **Wir wollen wandern gehen.** *(veer <u>vô</u>-len <u>vân</u>-
  dêrn <u>geh</u>-en)* (We want to go hiking)

✔ **Ich will bergsteigen.** *(îH vîl <u>bêrg</u>-shty-gen)* (I want to go rock climbing.)

✔ **Wir wollen im Herbst in die Dolomiten zum Bergsteigen.** *(veer <u>vô</u>-len îm hêrpst în dee dô-lô-<u>mee</u>-ten tsûm <u>bêrg</u>-shty-gen)* (We want to go mountain climbing in the Dolomite Alps in the fall.)

✔ **Wir werden in Berghütten übernachten.** *(veer <u>vêr</u>-den în <u>bêrg</u>-huu-tn uu-bêr-<u>nâH</u>-ten)* (We are going to stay in mountain huts.)

Words to Know

der Berg	dehr bêrg	mountain
das Gebirge	dâs ge-<u>bîr</u>-ge	mountain range
die Gegend	dee <u>geh</u>-gent	area
der Gipfel	dehr <u>gîp</u>-fel	peak
der Hügel	dehr <u>huu</u>-gel	hill
die Karte	dee <u>kâr</u>-te	map
das Naturschutz-gebiet	dâs nâ-<u>toor</u>-shûts-ge-<u>beet</u>	nature preserve
spazieren gehen	shpâ-<u>tsee</u>-ren gehn	to take a walk
das Tal	dâs tahl	valley
wandern	<u>vân</u>-dêrn	to go hiking
die Wanderung	dee <u>vân</u>-de-rûng	hike
der Weg	dehr vehgk	trail, path, way

Going to the country

If some fresh country air is your cup of tea, all you need to get started is the right language:

- ✔ **Wir fahren aufs Land.** *(veer fah-ren owfs länt)* (We are going to the country.)

- ✔ **Wir machen Urlaub auf dem Bauernhof.** *(veer mâ-Hn oor-lowp owf dehm bow-êrn-hohf)* (We are vacationing on a farm.)

- ✔ **Ich gehe im Wald spazieren.** *(îH geh-e îm vâlt shpâ-tsee-ren)* (I am going for a walk in the woods.)

- ✔ **der Bauernhof** *(dehr bow-êrn-hof)* (farm)

- ✔ **das Dorf** *(dâs dôrf)* (village)

- ✔ **das Feld** *(dâs fêlt)* (field)

- ✔ **das Land** *(dâs länt)* (countryside)

- ✔ **der Wald** *(dehr vâlt)* (forest)

- ✔ **die Wiese** *(dee vee-ze)* (meadow)

Going to the sea

If you decide to brave the wild North Sea or settle for the more serene Baltic Sea, you'll be able to enjoy nature and meet the locals at the same time using the following words:

- ✔ **die Ebbe** *(dee ê-be)* (low tide)

- ✔ **die Flut** *(dee floot)* (high tide)

- ✔ **die Gezeiten** *(dee gê-tsy-tn)* (tides)

- ✔ **die Küste** *(dee kuus-te)* (coast)

- ✔ **das Meer** *(dâs mehr)* (sea)

- ✔ **die Nordsee** *(dee nôrt-zeh)* (North Sea)

- ✔ **die Ostsee** *(dee ôst-zeh)* (Baltic Sea)

- ✔ **der Sturm** *(dehr shtûrm)* (storm)

- ✔ **die Welle** *(dee vê-le)* (wave)

- ✔ **der Wind** *(dehr vînt)* (wind)

Chapter 8

When You Gotta Work

In This Chapter

▶ Managing the telephone

▶ Sending a letter, fax, and e-mail

▶ Working around the office

Dealing with the phone, making appointments, and sending letters and e-mails are all part of a day's work. This chapter helps you get through that day in German.

Phoning Made Simple

When German speakers pick up **das Telefon** (*dâs tê-le-fohn*) (phone), they usually answer the call by stating their last name — particularly when they're at their office. If you call somebody at home, you sometimes may hear a simple **Hallo?** (*hâ-loh*) (*or:* *hâ-loh*) (Hello?).

If you want to express that you're going to call somebody or that you want somebody to call you, you use the verb **anrufen** (*ân-roo-fen*). It's a separable verb, so the prefix **an** (*ân*) gets separated from the stem **rufen** (*roo-fen*) (to call), when you conjugate it:

Conjugation	Pronunciation
ich rufe an	îH <u>roo</u>-fe ân
du rufst an	doo roofst ân
Sie rufen an	zee roofn ân

er, sie, es ruft an	ehr, zee, ês rooft ân
wir rufen an	veer roofn ân
ihr ruft an	eer rooft ân
Sie rufen an	zee roofn ân
sie rufen an	zee roofn ân

Asking for your party

To ask for your party, you have quite a few options:

- ✔ **Ich möchte gern Herrn / Frau . . . sprechen.**
  (îH muoH-te gêrn hêrn / frow . . . shprê-Hen)
  (I would like to talk to Mr. / Mrs. . . .)

- ✔ **Ist Herr / Frau . . . zu sprechen?** *(îst hêr / frow . . . tsoo shprê-Hen)* (Is Mr. / Mrs. . . . available?)

- ✔ **Kann ich bitte mit Herrn / Frau . . . sprechen?**
  (kân îH bî-te mît hêrn / frow . . . shprê-Hen)
  (Can I speak to Mr. / Mrs. . . . , please?)

- ✔ **Herrn / Frau . . . , bitte.** *(hêrn / frow . . . , bî-te)*
  (Mr. / Mrs. . . . , please.)

If you find that somebody talks too fast for you to understand, you can ask the person:

- ✔ **Können Sie bitte langsamer sprechen?** *(kuo-nen zee bî-te lâng-zah-mer sprê-Hen)* (Could you please talk more slowly?)

- ✔ **Können Sie das bitte wiederholen?** *(kuo-nen zee dâs bî-te vee-der-hoh-len)* (Could you repeat that, please?)

Making the connection

After you've asked to speak to a specific person, you could hear any number of responses depending on whom you're calling and where they are:

✔ **Am Apparat.** *(âm âpa-raht)* (Speaking.)

✔ **Einen Moment bitte, ich verbinde.** *(ay-nen moh-mênt bî-te, îH fêr-bîn-de)* (One moment please, I'll put you through.)

✔ **Er / sie telefoniert gerade.** *(ehr / zee tê-le-foh-neert ge-rah-de)* (He / she is on the phone right now.)

✔ **Die Leitung ist besetzt.** *(dee ly-tûng îst be-zêtst)* (The line is busy.)

✔ **Können Sie später noch einmal anrufen?** *(kuo-nen zee speh-ter nôH ayn-mahl ân-roo-fen)* (Could you call again later?)

✔ **Kann er / sie Sie zurückrufen?** *(kân ehr / zee zee tsoo-ruuk-roo-fen)* (Can he / she call you back?)

✔ **Hat er / sie Ihre Telefonnummer?** *(hât ehr / zee eeh-re tê-le-fohn-nû-mer)* (Does he / she have your phone number?)

Here are some helpful expressions if something goes wrong with your connection:

✔ **Es tut mir leid. Ich habe mich verwählt.** *(ês toot meer lyt. îH hah-be mîH fer-vehlt)* (I'm sorry. I have dialed the wrong number.)

✔ **Ich kann Sie schlecht verstehen.** *(îH kân zee shlêHt fêr-shtehn)* (I can't hear you very well.)

✔ **Er / sie meldet sich nicht.** *(ehr / zee mêl-det zîH nîHt)* (He / she doesn't answer the phone.)

Leaving messages

Unfortunately, you often don't get through to the person you're trying to reach, and you have to leave a message. In that case, some of the following expressions may come in handy:

✔ **Kann ich ihm / ihr eine Nachricht hinterlassen?** *(kân îH eem / eer ay-ne nahH-rîHt hîn-ter-lâsn)* (May I leave him / her a message?)

✔ **Kann ich ihm etwas ausrichten?** *(kân îH eem êt-vâs <u>ows</u>-rîH-ten)* (Can I leave him a message/take a message?)

✔ **Möchten Sie eine Nachricht hinterlassen?** *(<u>muoH</u>-ten zee <u>ay</u>-ne <u>naH</u>-rîHt hîn-ter-<u>lâsn</u>)* (Would you like to leave a message?)

✔ **Ich bin unter der Nummer . . . zu erreichen.** *(îH bîn <u>ûn</u>-ter dehr <u>nû</u>-mer . . . tsoo êr-<u>ry</u>-Hen)* (I can be reached at the number . . .)

Note that **ihm** *(eem)* and **ihr** *(eer)* are personal pronouns in the dative case. In German — as in English — you use the dative case of pronouns to express that you want to talk to or speak with a person (him or her):

Ich möchte gern mit ihm / ihr sprechen. *(îH <u>muoH</u>-te gêrn mît eem / eer <u>shprê</u>-Hen)* (I would like to speak with him / her.)

But watch out — in German, you don't leave a message *for* somebody; you just leave somebody a message:

Ich hinterlasse Ihnen / dir / ihm / ihr eine Nachricht. *(îH <u>hîn</u>-ter-<u>lâ</u>-se <u>ee</u>-nen / deer / eem / eer <u>ay</u>-ne <u>nahH</u>-rîHt)* (I'm leaving a message for you (formal / informal) / him / her.)

Saying good-bye

When saying good-bye on the phone, you say **auf Wiederhören!** *(owf <u>vee</u>-der-huo-ren!)* instead of **auf Wiedersehen** *(owf <u>vee</u>-der-zeh-en),* the expression you use if you say good-bye to somebody you've just seen in person. **Auf Wiedersehen** combines **wieder** *(<u>vee</u>-der)* (again) with the verb **sehen** *(<u>zeh</u>-en)* (to see), and **auf Wiederhören** uses the verb **hören** *(<u>huo</u>-ren)* (to hear), so it literally means "hear you again."

Take a look at the following dialog for a complete phone conversation:

Receptionist: **Firma TransEuropa, guten Tag!**
(*fĩr-mâ* *trâns-oy-roh-pâ, gûtn tahgk*) (TransEuropa
company, good day!)

Mr. Seibold: **Guten Tag, Seibold hier. Kann ich
bitte mit Herrn Huber sprechen?** (*gûtn tahgk,
zy-bôldt heer. kân ĩH bĩ-te mĩt hêrn hoo-ber shprê-
Hen*) (Good day, Seibold here. Can I please speak
to Mr. Huber?)

Receptionist: **Guten Tag, Herr Seibold. Einen
Moment bitte, ich verbinde.** (*gûtn tahgk, hêr zy-
bôldt. ay-nen moh-mênt bĩ-te, ĩH fêr-bĩn-de*) (Good
day, Mr. Seibold. One moment, please. I'll connect you.)

Receptionist: **Herr Seibold? Herr Huber spricht
gerade auf der anderen Leitung. Möchten Sie
ihm eine Nachricht hinterlassen?** (*hêr zy-bôldt?
hêr hoo-ber shprĩHt ge-rah-de owf dehr ân-de-ren
ly-tûngk. muoH-ten zee eem ay-ne nahH-rĩHt hĩn-
ter-lâssn*) (Mr. Seibold? Mr. Huber is on the other
line. Would you like to leave him a message?)

Mr. Seibold: **Ja bitte. Ich bin unter der Nummer
57 36 48 zu erreichen.** (*yah, bĩ-te. ĩH bĩn ûn-têr
dehr nû-mer fuunf zeebn dry zeks feer âHt tsoo êr-
ry-Hen*) (Yes, please. I can be reached at the
number 57 36 48.)

Receptionist: **Ich werde es ausrichten!** (*ĩH vehr-
de ês ows-rĩH-ten*) (I'll forward the message.)

Mr. Seibold: **Vielen Dank! Auf Wiederhören!**
(*vee-len dângk. owf vee-der-huo-ren*) (Thanks a
lot! Good-bye!)

Words to Know

der Anruf-beantworter	dehr ân-roof-be-ânt-vôrtr	answering machine
anrufen	ân-roo-fen	to call
		continued

Words to Know (continued)

das Telefon	dâs <u>tê</u>-le-fohn	phone
das Telefon-buch	dâs tê-le-<u>fohn</u>-booH	phone book
das Telefon-gespräch	dâs tê-le-<u>fohn</u>-ge-shprehH	phone call
die Telefon-nummer	dee <u>tê</u>-le-<u>fohn</u>-nû-mer	phone number
auf Wiederhören!	owf <u>vee</u>-der-<u>huo</u>-ren	Good-bye! (on the phone)
zurückrufen	tsoo-<u>ruuk</u>-roo-fen	to call back

Making Appointments

You hardly get to see anybody without making an appointment, so take a look at some of the vocabulary that may help you get through the door:

> ✔ **Ich möchte gern einen Termin machen.** *(îH <u>muoH</u>-te gêrn <u>ay</u>-nen têr-<u>meen</u> <u>mâ</u>-Hen)* (I would like to make an appointment.)

> ✔ **Kann ich meinen Termin verschieben?** *(kân îH <u>my</u>-nen têr-<u>meen</u> fêr-<u>shee</u>-ben)* (Can I change my appointment?)

And here are some of the answers you may hear:

> ✔ **Wann passt es Ihnen?** *(vân pâst ês <u>ee</u>-nen)* (What time suits you?)

> ✔ **Wie wäre es mit . . .?** *(vee <u>veh</u>-re ês mît . . .)* (How about . . .?)

> ✔ **Heute ist leider kein Termin mehr frei.** *(hoy-te îst ly-der kyn têr-meen mehr fry)* (Unfortunately, there is no appointment available today.)

The following dialog shows you how to make an appointment at the doctor's office:

Receptionist: **Praxis Dr. Eggert.** *(prâ-ksîs dôc-tôr ê-gert)* (Dr. Eggert's office.)

Anita: **Guten Tag, Anita Bauer. Ich möchte einen Termin für nächste Woche machen.** *(gûtn tahgk, â-nee-tâ bowr. îH muoH-te ay-nen têr-meen fuur nehH-ste vô-He mâ-Hen)* (Good day. This is Anita Bauer. I would like to make an appointment for next week.)

Receptionist: **Wann passt es Ihnen?** *(vân pâst ês ee-nen)* (What time suits you?)

Anita: **Mittwoch wäre gut.** *(mît-vôH veh-re goot)* (Wednesday would be good.)

Receptionist: **Mittwoch ist leider kein Termin mehr frei. Wie wäre es mit Donnerstag?** *(mît-vôH îst ly-der kyn têr-meen mehr fry. vee veh-re ês mît dônr-stahgk)* (Unfortunately, there is no appointment available on Wednesday. How about Thursday?)

Anita: **Donnerstag ist auch gut. Geht fünfzehn Uhr?** *(dônr-stahgk îst owH goot. geht fuunf-tsehn oor)* (Thursday is good, too. Does 3:00 p.m. work?)

Receptionist: **Kein Problem. Dann bis Donnerstag!** *(kyn proh-blehm. dân bîs dônr-stahgk)* (No problem. Until Thursday.)

Anita: **Bis dann. Auf Wiederhören.** *(bîs dân. owf vee-der-huo-ren)* (See you then. Good-bye.)

Sending a Letter, Fax, or E-Mail

Entire books have been written about the art of writing letters in German; in this section we just want to give you enough information so that you can send your correspondence where it needs to go.

Sending a letter or postcard

With people standing in line behind you, it pays to be prepared with some simple phrases that can get you in and out of the post office, **das Postamt** *(dâs pôst-âmt)*, as quickly and hassle-free as possible. (And get your letter, **der Brief** *[dehr breef]*, postcard, **die Postkarte** *[dee pôst-kâr-te]*, or package, **das Paket** *[dâs pâ-keht]*, on their merry way.)

- ✔ **Ich möchte gern Briefmarken kaufen.** *(îH muoH-te ger-n breef-mâr-kn kow-fen)* (I would like to buy stamps.)

- ✔ **Ich möchte diesen Brief per Eilzustellung / per Luftpost / per Einschreiben schicken.** *(îH muoH-te dee-zen breef pêr ayl-tsoo-shtê-lûngk / pêr lûft-pôst /pêr ayn-shrybn shî-ken)* (I would like to send this letter express / by air mail / by registered mail.)

- ✔ **Ich möchte dieses Paket aufgeben.** *(îH muoH-te dee-zes pâ-keht owf-geh-ben)* (I would like to send this package.)

Take a look at this conversation a woman has with **der Postbeamte** *(dehr pôst-be-âm-te)* (the postal worker):

Woman: **Guten Tag. Ich möchte den Einschreibebrief hier aufgeben. Wann kommt der Brief in München an?** *(gûtn tahgk. îH muoH-te dehn ayn-shry-be-breef heer owf-geh-ben. vân kômt dehr breef în muun-Hen ân)* (Good day. I would like to send this registered letter. When will the letter arrive in Munich?)

Postal clerk: **Heute ist Dienstag — vielleicht am Donnerstag, aber ganz bestimmt am Freitag.** *(hoy-te îst deens-tahgk — fee-lyHt âm dônr-stahgk, ah-ber gânts bê-shtîmt âm fry-tahgk)* (Today is Tuesday — perhaps on Thursday, but certainly on Friday.)

Woman: **Das ist zu spät. Kommt er übermorgen an, wenn ich ihn als Eilbrief schicke?** (*dâs îst tsoo shpait. kômt ehr <u>uuber</u>-môr-gn an, vên îH een âls <u>ayl</u>-breef <u>shî</u>-ke*) (That's too late. Will it arrive the day after tomorrow, if I send it as an express letter?)

Postal clerk: **Garantiert!** (*gârân-<u>teert</u>*) (Guaranteed.)

Woman: **Gut, dann schicken Sie das Einschreiben bitte per Eilzustellung.** (*goot, dân <u>shî</u>-ken zee dahs <u>ayn</u>-shry-ben <u>bî</u>-te pêr <u>ayl</u>-tsoo-shtê-lûng*) (Good, please send the registered letter per express.)

Words to Know

der Absender	dehr <u>âp</u>-zên-der	sender
der Briefkasten	dehr <u>breef</u>-kâstn	public mailbox
die Briefmarke	dee <u>breef</u>-mâr-ke	stamp
die Briefmarken	dee <u>breef</u>-mâr-kn	stamps
der Eilbrief	dehr <u>ayl</u>-breef	express letter
das Einschreiben	dâs <u>ayn</u>-shrybn	registered letter / certified mail
der Empfänger	dehr êm-<u>pfên</u>-ger	addressee
die Luftpost	dee <u>lûft</u>-pôst	airmail
das Paket	dâs pâ-<u>keht</u>	package
das Porto	dâs <u>pôr</u>-toh	postage

Sending a fax or an e-mail

If you need to use a fax machine — **das Faxgerät** *(dās fāks-ge-reht)* — here are a couple useful phrases:

> ✔ **Ich möchte etwas faxen.** *(īH muoH-te ĕt-vâss fāk-sen)* (I would like to fax something.)

> ✔ **Ich schicke Ihnen ein Fax.** *(īH shī-ke ee-nen ayn fāks)* (I'm sending you a fax.)

Knowing a few words connected with e-mailing is also important:

> ✔ **der Computer** *(dehr com-pjuh-ter)* (computer)

> ✔ **die E-mail** *(dee ee-mail)* (e-mail)

> ✔ **die E-mail-Adresse** *(dee ee-mail ah-drē-se)* (e-mail address)

> ✔ **das Internet** *(dās īn-ter-nêt)* (Internet)

> ✔ **Ich schicke eine E-mail.** *(īH shī-ke ay-ne ee-mail)* (I'm sending an e-mail.)

Getting Around at the Office

Germans have a reputation for being rather productive and efficient, but you might be surprised to find out that, statistically speaking, they don't work as much as Americans. Not that people never work late, but some businesses and state and government agencies, in particular, stick to a strict nine-to-five work schedule. And on Fridays, many companies close early.

When you're working in a German-speaking office, which is called **das Büro** *(dās buu-roh),* you'll give out assignments or receive them — **die Büroarbeit** *(dee buu-roh-âr-byt)* (office work).

You need to know the basics, such as what all the stuff on your desk or all the goodies in the supply closet are. After you can identify them, you need to know how to describe what to do with them. Time to get to work!

Mastering your desk and supplies

Typically, you may find, or hope to find, the following items on or around your desk, which is called **der Schreibtisch** *(dehr shryp-tĩsh)*:

- ✔ **der Brief** *(dehr breef)* (letter)
- ✔ **der Computer** *(dehr com-pjuh-ter)* (computer)
- ✔ **das Faxgerät** *(dâs fâks-gê-reht)* (fax machine)
- ✔ **der Kopierer** *(dehr kô-pee-rêr)* (copier)
- ✔ **die Schreibmaschine** *(dee shryp-mâ-shee-ne)* (typewriter)
- ✔ **das Telefon** *(dâs tê-le-fohn)* (telephone)
- ✔ **die Unterlagen** *(dee ûn-têr-lahgn)* (documents or files)

Don't forget the question **Wo ist . . . ?** *(voh ĩst)* (Where is . . . ?) if you need to ask someone for help finding something around the office.

Sooner or later, you're going to come up short of one of the following supplies:

- ✔ **der Bleistift** *(dehr bly-shtĩft)* (pencil)
- ✔ **der Briefbogen** *(dehr breef-boh-gn)* (letterhead)
- ✔ **der Kugelschreiber** *(dehr koo-gel-shry-ber)* (pen)
- ✔ **das Papier** *(dâs pâ-peer)* (paper)
- ✔ **der Umschlag** *(dehr ûm-shlahgk)* (envelope)

When you need some of these supplies and you can't find them on your own (you brave soul), you can ask a colleague to help you by saying:

✔ **Haben Sie einen Kugelschreiber / einen Umschlag für mich?** *(hah-ben zee ay-nen koo-gel-shry-ber / ay-nen ūm-shlahgk fuur mīH)* (Could you give me a pen / envelope. Literally: Do you have a pencil / envelope for me?)

✔ **Können Sie mir sagen, wo ich Umschläge / Briefbögen / Papier finde?** *(kuo-nen zee meer zah-gen, voh īH ūm-shlê-ge / breef-buo-gen / pâ-peer fīn-de)* (Could you tell me where I would find envelopes / stationery / paper?)

Elsewhere in the office . . .

Just as in English, German-speaking countries have their business world with its own culture and specialized language. Here are some common office terms:

✔ **anrufen** *(ān-roo-fen)* (to phone)

✔ **die Besprechung** *(dee be-shprê-Hūng)* (meeting)

✔ **der Chef / die Chefin** *(dehr shêf / die shê-fīn)* (boss)

✔ **faxen** *(fāk-sen)* (to fax)

✔ **diktieren** *(dīk-tee-ren)* (to dictate)

✔ **der Direktor / die Direktorin** *(dehr dî-rêk-tohr / dee dî-rêk-toh-rīn)* (director)

✔ **kopieren** *(kô-pee-ren)* (to copy)

✔ **der Mitarbeiter / die Mitarbeiterin** *(dehr mīt-âr-by-ter / dee mīt-âr-by-te-rīn)* (colleague / employee)

✔ **schicken** *(shī-ken)* (to send)

✔ **die Sekretärin / der Sekretär** *(dee zê-krê-teh-rīn / dehr zê-krê-tehr)* (secretary)

✔ **der Termin** *(dehr têr-meen)* (appointment)

Chapter 9

Getting Around: Transportation

. . . .

In This Chapter

▶ Choosing transportation

▶ Getting through customs

▶ Asking directions

▶ Driving yourself around

. . . .

*I*n this chapter, you're on the move on planes, trains, cars, and buses. We tell you what you need to know to deal with ticket agents, customs officials, a car-rental staff, and train and bus personnel. We also show you how to ask the occasional bystander for directions, all the while keeping a cool head, smiling, and being polite.

On the Move: Types of Transportation

You need to be able to get around with your language skills. The following sections give you some basic phrases to get you on the move.

At the airport

Most airline personnel speak several languages, so
they usually can assist you in English. Just to make
sure you know what you're holding in your hand, **das
Flugticket / der Flugschein** *(dâs floogk-tîket / dehr
floogk-shyn),* is your airplane ticket. It's probably a
Rückflugticket *(ruuk-floogk-tî-ket)* (a roundtrip ticket).
When you're checking in, the agent hands you your
die Bordkarte *(dee bôrd-kâr-te)* (boarding pass).

If you need to pick up your ticket, stop an attendant
and ask for directions or anything else you need to
know:

- ✔ **Wo ist der . . .-Schalter?** *(vô îst dehr . . . -shâl-ter)*
  (Where is the . . . counter?)

- ✔ **Ich möchte mein Ticket abholen.** *(îH muoH-te
  myn tî-ket âp-hoh-len)* (I would like to pick up my
  ticket.)

- ✔ **Wann muss ich einchecken?** *(vân mûs îH ayn-
  chê-kn)* (When do I have to check in?)

- ✔ **Wie viele Gepäckstücke kann ich mitnehmen?**
  (vee fee-le ge-pêk-stuu-ke kân îH mît-neh-men)
  (How many pieces of luggage can I take along?)

When you check in, the attendant asks you a few
questions to prepare you for boarding the plane:

- ✔ **Haben Sie Gepäck?** *(hah-bn zee ge-pêk)* (Do you
  have luggage?)

- ✔ **Wo möchten Sie sitzen, am Fenster oder am
  Gang?** *(vô muoH-ten zee zîtsn, âm fêns-ter oh-der
  âm gâng)* (Where would you like to sit, by the
  window or by the aisle?)

You may also want to ask the following to get some
details about the flight:

- ✔ **Wie lange dauert der Flug?** *(vee lân-ge dow-êrt
  dehr floogk)* (How long is the flight?)

- ✔ **Wann fliegt die Maschine ab?** *(vân fleekt dee
  mâ-shee-ne âp)* (When does the plane leave?)

If you're at the airport to meet somebody who is arriving on another plane, you can ask

Wann kommt die Maschine aus . . . an? *(vân kômt dee mâ-shee-ne ows . . . ân)* (When does the plane from . . . arrive?)

Words to Know

abfliegen	âp-flee-gen	to leave (on a plane)
der Abflug	dehr âp-floogk	departure
abholen	âp-hoh-len	to pick up
ankommen	ân-kô-men	to arrive
die Ankunft	dee ân-kûnft	arrival
einchecken	ayn-tshê-ken	to check in
fliegen	flee-gen	to fly
der Flug	dehr floogk	flight
der Flugsteig	dehr floogk-shtyk	gate
das Flugzeug / die Maschine	das floogk-tsoyg / dee mâ-shee-ne	airplane
das Gepäck / Handgepäck	dâs ge-pêk / hând-ge-pêk	luggage / hand luggage
pünktlich	puunkt-lîH	on time
verspätet	fêr-shpeh-tet	delayed

At the train station

Every train station displays schedules for all the trains that run through that particular station. The following expressions can provide some guidance for demystifying train schedules:

- ✔ **die Abfahrt** *(dee _âp_-fahrt)* (departure)
- ✔ **die Ankunft** *(dee _ân_-kûnft)* (arrival)
- ✔ **der Fahrplan** *(dehr _fahr_-plahn)* (train schedule)
- ✔ **sonn- und feiertags** *(_zôn_ ûnt _fy_-êr-tâhks)* (Sundays and holidays)
- ✔ **über** *(_uu_-ber)* (via)
- ✔ **werktags** *(_vêrk_-tâks)* (workdays)

When you have questions about a train you want to take, head to the information counter, **die Auskunft** *(dee _ows_-kûnft)*. There, you may need to ask any of the following questions:

- ✔ **Von welchem Gleis fährt der Zug nach . . . ab?**
  (fôn _vêl_-Hem glys fehrt dehr tsoog nahH . . . ap)
  (Which track does the train to . . . leave from?)

- ✔ **Auf welchem Gleis kommt der Zug aus . . . an?**
  (fôn _vêl_-Hem glys kômt dehr tsoog ows . . . ân)
  (Which track does the train from . . . arrive on?)

- ✔ **Hat der Zug Verspätung?** *(hât dehr tsoog fêr-_shpeh_-tûng)* (Is the train delayed?)

- ✔ **Gibt es einen direkten Zug von . . . nach . . .?**
  (gîpt ês _ay_-nen dî-_rêk_-ten tsoog fôn . . . nahh)
  (Is there a direct train from . . . to . . .?)

The answer to most of these questions will be straightforward — but you may hear that no direct trains are available:

Nein, Sie müssen in . . . umsteigen. *(nyn, zee _muu_-sn în . . . _ûm_-shty-gen)* (No, you have to change trains in . . .)

Words to Know

abfahren	<u>âp</u>-fah-ren	leave
ankommen	<u>ân</u>-kô-men	arrive
aussteigen	<u>ows</u>-shty-gen	get off
der Bahnsteig	dehr <u>bahn</u>-shtyk	platform
einsteigen	<u>ayn</u>-shty-gen	get on
fahren	<u>fah</u>-ren	go by
das Gleis	dâs glys	track
umsteigen	<u>ûm</u>-shty-gen	change (trains, buses, and so on)
die Verspätung	dee fêr-<u>shpeh</u>-tûng	delay
die Zugver-bindung	dee <u>tsuhgk</u>-fêr-bîn-dûng	the train connection

For tickets, you need to go to the ticket booth, **der Fahrkartenschalter** *(dehr fahr-kâr-ten-<u>shâl</u>-ter)*. With the help of these words, you can go anywhere.

- ✔ **Eine Fahrkarte nach . . . , bitte.** *(<u>ay</u>-ne <u>fahr</u>-kâr-te nahH . . . , <u>bî</u>-te)* (A train ticket to . . . please.)

- ✔ **Einfach oder hin und zurück?** *(<u>ayn</u>-fâH <u>oh</u>-der hîn ûnt tsû-<u>ruuk</u>)* (One-way or roundtrip?)

- ✔ **Was kostet eine Rückfahrkarte nach . . .?** *(vâs <u>kôs</u>-tet <u>ay</u>-ne <u>ruuk</u>-fahr-kâr-te nahH . . .)* (How much does a roundtrip ticket to . . . cost?)

- ✔ **Was kostet eine einfache Fahrt nach . . .?** *(vâs <u>kôs</u>-tet <u>ay</u>-ne <u>ayn</u>-fâ-He fahrt nahH . . .)* (How much does a one-way ticket to . . . cost?)

✔ **Erster oder zweiter Klasse?** _(ehrs-ter oh-der tsvy-ter klâ-se?)_ (In first or second class?)

✔ **Ich möchte gern eine Platzkarte für den . . . von . . . nach . . .** _(îH muoH-te gêrn ay-ne plâts-kâr-te fuur dehn . . . fôn . . . naH . . .)_ (I would like to reserve a seat on the . . . [insert train name or number here] from . . . to . . .)

Words to Know

einfach	<u>ayn</u>-fâH	one-way
die erste Klasse	dee <u>êrs</u>-te <u>klâ</u>-se	first class
die Fahrkarte	dee <u>fahr</u>-kâr-te	train ticket
hin und zurück	hîn ûnt tsû-<u>ruuk</u>	roundtrip
die Platzkarte	dee <u>plâts</u>-kâr-te	reserved seat
die zweite Klasse	dee <u>tsvy</u>-te <u>klâ</u>-se	second class

Catching the bus

If you need help finding the right **Bus** _(bûs)_ (bus) to take, you may ask at the **Fahrkartenschalter** _(fahr-kârtn-shâl-ter)_ (ticket window), or any bus driver **(der Busfahrer)** _(dehr bûs-fah-rer)_ any of the following questions:

✔ **Welche Buslinie fährt ins Stadtzentrum?** _(<u>vêl</u>-He <u>bûs</u>-lîn-ye fehrt îns <u>shtât</u>-tsên-trûm)_ (Which bus line goes to the city center?)

✔ **Ist das die richtige Straßenbahn zum Stadion?** _(îst dâs dee <u>rîH</u>-tee-ge <u>shtrah</u>-sn-bahn tsûm <u>shtah</u>-dî-on)_ (Is this the right streetcar to the stadium?)

✔ **Muss ich umsteigen?** _(mûs îH <u>ûm</u>-shty-gen)_ (Do I have to switch buses?)

✔ **Hält diese U-Bahn am Hauptbahnhof?** *(hêlt dee-ze oo-bahn âm howpt-bahn-hohf)* (Does this subway stop at the main train station?)

✔ **Wie viele Haltestellen sind es bis zum Goetheplatz?** *(vee fee-le hâl-te-shtê-len zînt ês bîs tsûm guo-te-plâts)* (How many stops are there to Goethe Square?)

✔ **Entschuldigen Sie bitte, hält hier die Buslinie 9?** *(ênt-shûl-dee-gen zee bî-te, hêlt heer dee bûs-leen-ye noyn)* (Excuse me please. Does the bus number 9 stop here?)

Words to Know

der Bus	dehr bûs	bus
die Buslinie / U-Bahnlinie	dee bûs-leen-ye / oo-bahn-leen-ye	bus line / subway line
der Fahrschein-automat	dehr fahr-shyn-ow-tô-maht	ticket vending machine
halten	hâl-ten	to stop
die Haltestelle	dee hâl-te-shtê-le	station, stop
die S-Bahn	dee ês-bahn	local train
die Straßen-bahn	dee shtrah-sn-bahn	streetcar
das Taxi	dâs tâk-see	taxi
der Taxistand	dehr tâk-see-shtânt	taxi stand
die U-bahn	dee oo-bahn	subway
die U-Bahn-station	dee oo-bahn-shtâts-yohn	subway station

Getting a taxi

Taking a taxi isn't hard. Just make your way over to the nearest **Taxistand** (_tāk-see-shtānt_) (taxi stand) and go straight up to the first car in the line. When you get in, the taxi driver (**Taxifahrer**) (_tāk-see-fah-rer_) will turn on the meter, and you pay the price indicated on the meter when you reach your destination.

To ask for the nearest taxi stand, just say the following:

> **Wo ist der nächste Taxistand?** (_vô īst dehr naiH-ste tāk-see-shtānt_) (Where is the closest taxi stand?)

After you're in the cab, the driver might ask

> **Wohin möchten Sie?** (_vô-hīn muoH-ten zee_) (Where would you like to go?)

Renting a car

If you've decided to rent a car, you need to make your way to the **Autovermietung** (_ow-tô-fêr-mee-tūng_) (car-rental agency). When you arrive at the car-rental agency, you can start out by saying

> **Ich möchte ein Auto mieten.** (_īH muoH-te ayn ow-tô mee-tn_) (I would like to rent a car.)

The attendant will ask you questions about what kind of car you want by saying something like

> **Was für ein Auto möchten Sie?** (_vâs fuur ayn ow-tô muoH-ten zee_) (What kind of car would you like?)

To which you can respond with any of the following:

- ✔ **einen Automatikwagen** (_ay-nen ow-tô-mah-tīk-vah-gen_) (car with automatic transmission)
- ✔ **einen Kombi** (_ay-nen kôm-bī_) (station wagon)
- ✔ **einen Schaltwagen** (_ay-nen shâlt-vah-gen_) (car with stick shift)

✔ **ein zweitüriges / viertüriges Auto** *(ayn tsvy-tuu-rî-ges / feer-tuu-rî-ges ow-tô)* (a two-door / four-door car)

You may also be asked

✔ **Für wie lange möchten Sie den Wagen mieten?** *(fuur vee lân-ge muoH-ten zee dehn vah-gen mee-tên)* (For how long would you like to rent the car?)

✔ **Ab wann möchten Sie den Wagen mieten?** *(âp vân muoH-ten zee dehn vah-gen mee-ten)* (Starting when would you like to rent the car?)

✔ **Bis wann möchten Sie den Wagen mieten?** *(bîs vân muoH-ten zee dehn vah-gen mee-ten)* (Until when would you like to rent the car?)

✔ **Wann / Wo möchten Sie den Wagen zurückgeben?** *(vân / vô muoH-ten zee dehn vah-gen tsû-ruuk-geh-ben)* (Where / When would you like to return the car?)

To which you can answer

✔ **Ich brauche den Wagen für . . .** *(îH brow-He dehn vah-gen fuur . . .)* (I need the car for . . .)

✔ **Ich möchte den Wagen ab dem . . . mieten.** *(îH muoH-te dehn vah-gen âp dehm . . . mee-ten)* (I would like to rent the car starting . . .)

✔ **Ich möchte den Wagen bis zum . . . mieten.** *(îH muoH-te dehn vah-gen bîs tsûm . . . mee-ten)* (I would like to rent the car until the . . .)

✔ **Ich möchte den Wagen am . . . zurückgeben.** *(îH muoH-te dehn vah-gen âm . . . tsû-ruuk-geh-ben)* (I would like to return the car on the . . .)

✔ **Ich möchte den Wagen in . . . zurückgeben.** *(îH muoH-te dehn vah-gen în . . . tsû-ruuk-geh-ben)* (I would like to return the car in . . .)

During the rental process, you'll hear the following words spoken:

- ✔ **der Führerschein** *(dehr <u>fuu</u>-rer-shyn)* (driver's license)

- ✔ **inbegriffen** *(<u>în</u>-be-grîfn)* (included)

- ✔ **ohne Kilometerbegrenzung** *(<u>oh</u>-ne kî-lô-<u>meh</u>-ter-be-<u>grên</u>-tsûng)* (unlimited mileage)

- ✔ **die Vollkaskoversicherung** *(dee <u>fôl</u>-kâs-kô-fêr-<u>zî</u>-He-rûng)* (full insurance)

Dealing with Passports, Visas, and Customs

Although the world is getting smaller through telecommunications and virtual travel, you still need paperwork to go places. This section gets you through passports, visas, and customs in German.

Your passport and visa

Before you leave on a trip, you want to check to make sure that your passport is valid for the entire length of your stay. If you forget to take care of this very important chore, you'll hear the following when you show your passport at the border:

Ihr Pass ist abgelaufen! *(eer pâs îst <u>âp</u>-ge-low-fn)* (Your passport has expired!)

In the event that you notice your passport is missing, head straight to the American consulate, **das amerikanische Konsulat** *(dâs â-mê-ree-<u>kah</u>-nî-she kôn-zû-<u>laht</u>)*, to report it:

Ich habe meinen Pass verloren. *(îH <u>hah</u>-be <u>my</u>-nen pâs fêr-<u>loh</u>-ren)* (I lost my passport.)

Don't forget to check whether you need a visa. If you do, the following phrases will come in handy:

- ✔ **Braucht man ein Visum für Reisen nach . . .?**
  (browHt mân ayn <u>vee</u>-zûm fuur <u>ry</u>-zn nahH . . .)
  (Does one need a visa for trips to . . .?)

✔ **Wie lange ist das Visum gültig?** *(vee lân-ge îst dâs vee-zûm guul-tîg)* (For how long is the visa valid?)

✔ **Wer stellt das Visum aus?** *(vehr shtêlt dâs vee-zûm ows)* (Who issues the visa?)

✔ **Ich möchte ein Visum beantragen.** *(îH muoH-te ayn vee-zûm bê-ân-trah-gen)* (I would like to apply for a visa.)

WORDS TO KNOW

ablaufen	âp-low-fen	to expire
beantragen	bê-ân-trah-gen	to apply for
die Botschaft	dee boht-shâft	embassy
gültig / ungültig	guul-tîg / ûn-guul-tîg	valid / invalid
das Konsulat	dâs kôn-zû-laht	consulate
der Reisepass	dehr ry-ze-pâs	passport
verlängern	fêr-lêng-êrn	to renew, to extend
das Visum	dâs vee-zûm	visa

Going through immigration

When you're getting off a transatlantic flight, you'll usually be directed straight to passport control, **die Passkontrolle** *(dee pâs-kôn-trô-le)*. Most of the time you get to choose between two lines: one is for **EU-Bürger** *(eh-oo-buur-ger)* (citizens of countries within the European Union) and the other is for **Nicht-EU-Bürger** *(nîHt-eh-oo-buur-ger)* (citizens of countries outside the EU).

These are the words you may need to wield when you go through passport control:

- ✔ **der Reisepass / der Pass** *(dehr <u>ry</u>-ze-pâs/ dehr pâs)* (passport)

- ✔ **EU-Bürger** *(eh-<u>oo</u>-<u>buur</u>-ger)* (citizen of a country of the European Union)

- ✔ **Nicht-EU-Bürger** *(<u>nîHt</u>-eh-oo-buur-ger)* citizen of a country outside the EU)

- ✔ **Ich bin im Urlaub hier.** *(îH bîn îm <u>ûr</u>-lowp heer)* (I'm here on vacation.)

- ✔ **Ich bin geschäftlich hier.** *(îH bîn ge-<u>shêft</u>-lîH heer)* (I'm here on business.)

- ✔ **Ich bin auf der Durchreise nach . . .** *(îH bîn owf dehr <u>dûrH</u>-ry-ze nâH . . .)* (I am on my way to . . .)

Going through customs

After passing through passport control, you claim your baggage and go through customs, **der Zoll** *(dehr tsôl)*. You usually either pick the line for people who have to declare goods — **anmeldepflichtige Waren** *(<u>ân</u>-mêl-de-pflîH-tee-ge <u>vah</u>-ren)* — or the line for no declaration. Those goodies are called **anmeldefreie Waren** *(<u>ân</u>-mêl-de-fry-e <u>vah</u>-ren)*. Here are some questions a customs officer may ask you:

Haben Sie etwas zu verzollen? *(<u>hah</u>-bn zee êt-vâs tsû fêr-<u>tsô</u>-len)* (Do you have anything to declare?)

Haben Sie etwas anzumelden? *(<u>hah</u>-bn zee êt-vâs <u>ân</u>-tsû-mêl-den)* (Do you have anything to declare?)

Bitte öffnen Sie diesen Koffer / diese Tasche. *(<u>bî</u>-te <u>uof</u>-nen zee <u>dee</u>-zn <u>kô</u>-fer / <u>dee</u>-ze <u>tâ</u>-she)* (Please open this suitcase / bag.)

To these questions, you can respond with the following:

- ✔ **Ich möchte . . . anmelden.** *(îH <u>muoH</u>-te . . . <u>ân</u>-mêl-den)* (I would like to declare . . .)

✔ **Ich habe nichts zu verzollen.** *(īH hah-be nīHts tsū fêr-tsô-len)* (I have nothing to declare.)

✔ **Es ist für meinen persönlichen Gebrauch.** *(ês īst fuur my-nen pêr-suon-līHen ge-browH)* (It's for my personal use.)

✔ **Es ist ein Geschenk.** *(ês īst ayn ge-shênk)* (It's a gift.)

Asking for Help with Directions

Asking for directions in German is fairly easy. The secret to finding a location is the word **wo** *(voh)* (where). The question you want to ask starts with

Wo ist . . .? *(voh īst . . .)* (Where is . . .?)

At the end of the sentence, just supply the name of the location that you're looking for, which could include any of the following:

✔ **die U-Bahnhaltestelle** *(dee oo-bahn-hâl-te-shtê-le)* (subway station)

✔ **der Bahnhof** *(dehr bahn-hohf)* (train station)

✔ **die Bank** *(dee bânk)* (bank)

✔ **die Bushaltestelle** *(dee bûs-hâl-te-shtê-le)* (bus stop)

✔ **der Flughafen** *(dehr floogk-hah-fen)* (airport)

✔ **der Hafen** *(dehr hah-fen)* (harbor)

✔ **das Hotel** *(dâs hoh-têl)* (hotel)

✔ **die Kirche** *(dee kîr-He)* (church)

✔ **der Markt** *(dehr mârkt)* (market)

✔ **das Museum** *(dâs mû-zeh-ûm)* (museum)

✔ **der Park** *(dehr pârk)* (park)

✔ **die Post** *(dee pôst)* (post office)

✔ **der Taxistand** *(dehr tâk-see-shtânt)* (taxi stand)

✔ **das Theater** *(dâs teh-ah-ter)* (theater)

If you want the closest location, you just insert **näch-ste** *(naiH-ste)* (closest) after the article of the location you're looking for. Check out a few examples of **nächste:**

- ✔ **Wo ist der nächste Park?** *(voh īst dehr naiH-ste pârk)* (Where is the closest park?)

- ✔ **Wo ist die nächste Bushaltestelle?** *(voh īst dee naiH-ste būs-hâl-te-shtê-le)* (Where is the closest bus stop?)

- ✔ **Wo ist das nächste Hotel?** *(voh īst dâs naiH-ste hoh-têl)* (Where is the closest hotel?)

You have a couple other options to find out if something is located in the vicinity or far away, and the key words to know are **nah** *(nah)* (close, near) / **Nähe** *(nai-he)* (vicinity) and **weit** *(vyt)* (far).

Ist . . . weit entfernt? *(īst . . . vyt ênt-fêrnt)* (Is . . . far away?)

Ist . . . in der Nähe? *(īst . . . īn dehr nai-he)* (Is . . . in the vicinity?)

Going Here and There

The words **hier** *(heer)* (here) and **dort** *(dôrt)* (there) often play an important part in communicating directions. They make directions just a little more specific. Look at the following sample sentences to see how **hier** and **dort** work in directions:

- ✔ **Das Museum ist nicht weit von hier.** *(dâs mū-zeh-ûm īst nīHt vyt fôn heer)* (The museum isn't far from here.)

- ✔ **Der Park ist nicht weit von dort.** *(dehr pârk īst nīHt vyt fôn dôrt)* (The park isn't far from there.)

A common expression you may hear is

Das ist gleich hier vorne / dort drüben. *(dâs īst glyH heer fôr-ne / dôrt druu-ben)* (That is right here / over there.)

Although "right here" and "over there" are the most common combinations, you also may hear

Das ist gleich hier drüben. *(dâs îst glyH heer <u>druu</u>-ben)* (That is right over here.)

The expressions **dort drüben** and **hier drüben** are practically interchangeable.

Asking "How Do 1 Get There?"

When you want to ask, "How do I get there?", you use the verb **kommen** *(<u>kô</u>-men),* which means both "to come" and, when used with a preposition, "to get to." (See Chapter 4 for the conjugation of **kommen.**)

The basic form of the question "How do I get there?" is

Wie komme ich . . .? *(vee <u>kô</u>-me îH . . .)* (How do I get . . .?)

To finish the rest of the sentence, you need to use a preposition — to help you say "*to* the train station" or "*to* the hotel." In German, you need to use any of a number of prepositions, all of which can mean "to." The most commonly used "to" prepositions are the following:

- ✔ **in** *(în)*
- ✔ **nach** *(nahH)*
- ✔ **zu** *(tsû)*

Describing a Position or Location

After you ask for directions, you must be ready to understand the possible answers. The German language uses quite a few prepositions to describe locations in this way. All these prepositions use the dative case in this context, just like **zu** in the previous section.

Table 9-1 shows you some common prepositions that are used to express the location of one thing in relation to another.

Table 9-1	**Prepositions that Express Locations**		
Preposition	*Pronunciation*	*Meaning*	*Example*
auf	owf	on	auf der Museumstraße (owf dehr mû-<u>zeh</u>-ûms-<u>shtrah</u>-se) on Museum Street
bei	by	near / next to	beim Bahnhof (bym <u>bahn</u>-hohf) near to the train station
hinter	hîn-ter	behind	hinter der Kirche (<u>hîn</u>-ter dehr <u>kîr</u>-He) behind the church
vor	fohr	in front of	vor der Post (fohr dehr pôst) in front of the post office
neben	<u>neh</u>-bn	next to	neben der Bank (<u>neh</u>-bn dehr bânk) next to the bank
zwischen	tsvî-shen	between	zwischen dem Theater und der Bank (<u>tsvî</u>-shen dehm teh-<u>ah</u>-ter ûnt dehr bânk) between the theater and the bank
gegenüber	geh-gen-<u>uu</u>-ber	opposite	gegenüber dem Museum (geh-gen-<u>uu</u>-ber dehm mû-<u>zeh</u>-ûm) opposite the museum

Preposition	Pronunciation	Meaning	Example
an	ân	at	an der Ecke (ân dehr ê-ke) at the corner

Here are a few of these prepositions in action:

✔ **Entschuldigen Sie bitte, wo ist der nächste Taxistand?** (*ênt-shûl-dî-gen zee bî-te, voh îst dehr naiH-ste tâk-see-shtant*) (Excuse me, where is the closest taxi stand?)

✔ **Sehen Sie die Kirche an der Ecke? Neben der Kirche ist ein Park und direkt gegenüber ist der Taxistand.** (*zehn zee dee kîr-He ân dehr ê-ke? neh-bn dehr kîr-He îst ein pârk ûnt dee-rêkt geh-gen-uu-ber îst dehr tâk-see-shtânt*) (Do you see the church at the corner? Next to the church is a park and directly opposite is the taxi stand.)

Going Right, Left, North, South, East, and West

When it comes to asking for or giving directions in German, there's no way to get around the key words for defining position: left and right.

✔ **links** (*lînks*) (left)

✔ **rechts** (*rêHts*) (right)

If you want to express that something is located to the left or right of something else, you add the preposition **von** (*fôn*) (of), making the following:

✔ **links von** (*lînks fôn*) (to the left of): For example — **Das Museum ist links von der Kirche.** (*dâs mû-zeh-ûm îst lînks fôn dehr kîr-He*) (The museum is to the left of the church.)

> ✔ **rechts von** *(rêHts fôn)* (to the right of): For
> example — **Die Kirche ist rechts vom Theater.**
> *(dee kîr-He îst rêHts fôm teh-ah-ter)* (The church
> is to the right of the theater.)

You may also hear the word **die Seite** *(dee zy-te)*
(side), when talking about directions. For example:

> ✔ **Das Museum ist auf der linken Seite.** *(dâs mû-*
> *zeh-ûm îst owf dehr lîng-ken zy-te)* (The museum
> is on the left side.)

> ✔ **Die Kirche ist auf der rechten Seite.** *(dee kîr-He*
> *îst owf dehr rêH-ten zy-te)* (The church is on the
> right side.)

The cardinal points also come in handy when you need
to define your position (or the position of something):

> ✔ **der Norden** *(dehr nôr-den)* (North)

> ✔ **der Süden** *(dehr zuu-den)* (South)

> ✔ **der Osten** *(dehr ôs-ten)* (East)

> ✔ **der Westen** *(dehr vês-ten)* (West)

To describe a position, you combine these with the
preposition **im** *(îm)*. For example:

> **Der Hafen liegt im Norden** *(dehr hah-fen leegkt*
> *îm nôr-den)* / **Süden** *(zuu-den)* / **Osten** *(ôs-ten)* /
> **Westen** *(wês-ten)*. (The harbor lies in the North /
> South / East / West).

Getting on the Move

If you've asked somebody for directions, you may
very well get the answer that you should take a specific street — the second street on the left or the first
street on the right, for example.

The verbs you need to be familiar with in this context
are **gehen** *(gehn)* (to go) and **nehmen** *(neh-men)* (to
take). In order to give directions, you use the impera-
tive. The verb goes at the beginning of the sentence.
For example:

> ✔ **Nehmen Sie die zweite Straße links!** (*neh-men zee dee tsvy-te shtrah-se lînks*) (Take the second street on the left.)

> ✔ **Gehen Sie die erste Straße rechts!** (*gehn zee dee êrs-te shtrah-se rêHts*) (Take the first street on the right.)

If you're looking for a specific building, you may hear something like

Es ist das dritte Haus auf der linken Seite. (*ês îst dâs drî-te hows owf dehr lîng-ken zy-te*) (It is the third house on the left side.)

And if you don't have to make a left or right but simply have to go straight on, you may hear the instruction:

Gehen Sie geradeaus! (*gehn zee grah-de-ows*) (Go straight ahead.)

Driving Around in German

In English, it doesn't make a big difference if you're going by car or on foot. Unfortunately, the German verb **gehen** (*gehn*) (to go) isn't that flexible. You may go on foot — **zu Fuß gehen** (*tsû fuhs gehn*) — but if you take the car, you're driving, — **fahren** (*fah-ren*) — not going.

When using **fahren** in a sentence, you need three things:

> ✔ The word for the type of vehicle you're using

> ✔ The preposition **mit** (*mît*) (with)

> ✔ The dative version of the vehicle's article

Here are a few examples of how you use the verb **fahren** in a sentence to say that you're taking a specific kind of transportation:

Ich fahre mit dem Auto. (*îH fah-re mît dehm ow-tô*) (I'm going by car. *Literally:* I'm driving with the car.)

To tell somebody to make a left or right turn, you can use your old friend, the verb **fahren.** You say

Fahren Sie links / rechts! *(<u>fah</u>-ren zee lĩnks / rêHts)* (Go left / right. *Literally:* Drive left / right.)

You can also use the verb **abbiegen** *(<u>âp</u>-beegn)* (to make a turn) to instruct somebody to make a left or right turn.

Biegen Sie links / rechts ab! *(<u>bee</u>-gn zee lĩnks / rêHts âp)* (Make a left / right turn!)

If you've lost your way driving around, memorize this expression:

Ich habe mich verfahren. Ich suche . . . *(îH <u>hah</u>-be mîH fêr-<u>fah</u>-ren. îH <u>zoo</u>-He . . .)* (I've lost my way. I'm looking for . . .)

When you're driving around on your own, knowing how to read a map is very helpful. Here are some of the maps you may want:

- ✔ **die Landkarte** *(dee <u>lânt</u>-kâr-te)* (map)
- ✔ **der Stadtplan** *(dehr <u>shtât</u>-plahn)* (map of a city)
- ✔ **die Straßenkarte** *(dee <u>shtrah</u>-sn-kâr-te)* (road map)

On a map written in German, you may see the following words:

- ✔ **die Altstadt** *(dee <u>âlt</u>-shtât)* (old town)
- ✔ **die Auffahrt** *(dee <u>owf</u>-fahrt)* (entrance ramp)
- ✔ **die Ausfahrt** *(dee <u>ows</u>-fahrt)* (exit ramp)
- ✔ **die Autobahn** *(dee <u>ow</u>-tô-bahn)* (freeway)
- ✔ **das Autobahndreieck** *(dâs <u>ow</u>-tô-bahn-<u>dry</u>-êk)* (three-freeway junction)
- ✔ **das Autobahnkreuz** *(dâs <u>ow</u>-tô-bahn-kroyts)* (two-freeway junction)
- ✔ **die Fußgängerzone** *(dee <u>foos</u>-gên-ger-<u>tsoh</u>-ne)* (pedestrian zone)

✔ **die Kirche** *(dee kîr-He)* (church)

✔ **der Parkplatz** *(dehr pârk-pláts)* (parking area)

Here are some of the most common road signs that you encounter in German-speaking countries:

✔ **50 bei Nebel** *(fuunf-tsîgk by neh-bel)* (50 km/h when foggy)

✔ **Anlieger frei** *(ân-lee-ger fry)* (access only; no exit)

✔ **Baustelle** *(bow-shtê-le)* (construction site)

✔ **Einbahnstraße** *(ayn-bahn-shtrah-se)* (one-way street)

✔ **Einordnen** *(ayn-ôrd-nen)* (merge)

✔ **Gesperrt** *(ge-shpêrt)* (closed)

✔ **Licht an / aus** *(lîHt ân / ows)* (lights on / off)

✔ **Umleitung** *(ûm-ly-tûng)* (detour)

✔ **Vorsicht Glätte** *(fohr-zîHt glê-te)* (slippery when wet)

Chapter 10

Finding a Place to Lay Your Weary Head

. . . .

In This Chapter
▶ Finding a hotel
▶ Making reservations
▶ Checking in: names, addresses, and room numbers
▶ Checking out and paying the bill

. . . .

*W*hether you've been working at the office, shopping, or traveling, at the end of the day, you need a place to lay your head. This chapter gives you the phrases you need to find a hotel.

Scoping Out a Hotel

The basic word for hotel in German is **das Hotel** *(dâs hoh-tēl)*. You can find a wide variety of hotels in German-speaking countries that offer different atmospheres and levels of service. In rural areas and smaller towns, hotels are often labeled a little differently. For example, the following types of hotels are common:

▶ **die Ferienwohnung** *(dee feh-rî-ên-voh-nûng)* (A "vacation apartment," a furnished apartment in holiday resorts)

▶ **das Gasthaus / der Gasthof** *(dâs gâst-hows / dehr gâst-hohf)* (An inn providing food and drinks and often lodging)

✔ **das Hotel garni** *(dâs hoh-__têl__ gâr-__nee__)* (A hotel that serves only breakfast)

✔ **die Jugendherberge** *(die __yoo__-gênt-hêr-bêr-ge)* (A youth hostel; in Austria, Germany, and Switzerland, youth hostels are quite comfortable and sometimes pretty upscale.)

✔ **die Pension** *(dee pâng-__zîohn__)* or **das Fremdenzimmer** *(dâs __frêm__-den-tsî-mer)* (A boardinghouse offering full board — breakfast, lunch, and dinner — or half board — breakfast, lunch, or dinner. Meals are usually served to houseguests only.)

✔ **der Rasthof / das Motel** *(dehr __râst__-hohf / dâs moh-__têl__)* (A roadside lodge, or motel, located just off an expressway)

Reserving Rooms

Reservations for hotel rooms are usually made over the telephone, so you may want to read Chapter 8 before you pick up the phone. When the hotel picks up the phone, you can say the following to announce the purpose of your call:

Ich möchte gern ein Zimmer reservieren. *(îH __muoH__-te gêrn ayn __tsî__-mer rê-zêr-__vee__-ren)* (I would like to reserve a room.)

The hotel clerk will likely ask

Von wann bis wann möchten Sie ein Zimmer reservieren? *(fôn vân bîs vân __muoH__-ten zee ayn __tsî__-mer __rê__-zêr-__vee__-ren)* (For what dates would you like to reserve a room?)

In order to specify how many nights you want to stay or for what dates you want to reserve, you could say either of the following:

✔ **Ich möchte gern ein Zimmer für . . . Nächte reservieren.** *(îH __muoH__-te gêrn ayn __tsî__-mer fuur . . . naiH-te rê-zêr-__vee__-ren)* (I would like to reserve a room for . . . nights.)

✔ **Ich möchte gern ein Zimmer vom 11. 3. bis zum 15. 3. reservieren.** *(îH muoH-te gêrn ayn tsî-mer fôm êlf-ten drî-ten bîs tsûm fuunf-tsehn-ten drî-ten rê-zêr-vee-ren)* (I would like to reserve a room from the 11th to the 15th of March.)

The person taking your reservation will certainly ask what kind of room you want:

Was für ein Zimmer möchten Sie gern? *(vâs fuur ayn tsî-mer muoH-ten zee gêrn)* (What kind of room would you like?)

You can take the initiative and state what kind of room you want with the phrase

Ich hätte gern . . . *(îH ha-te gêrn . . .)* (I would like . . .)

At the end of the phrase, substitute any of the following (or combination of the following):

✔ **ein Doppelzimmer** *(ayn dôpl-tsî-mer)* (a double room)

✔ **ein Einzelzimmer** *(ayn ayn-tsêl-tsî-mer)* (a single room)

✔ **ein Zimmer mit . . .** *(ayn tsî-mer mît . . .)* (a room with . . .)

• **Bad** *(baht)* (bathtub)

• **Dusche** *(doo-she)* (shower)

• **einem Doppelbett** *(ay-nêm dôpl-bêt)* (one double bed)

• **zwei Einzelbetten** *(tsvy ayn-tsêl-bê-ten)* (two twin beds)

You also want to find out what the hotel room costs. These are some possible ways to ask the question, depending on whether you want to know the basic price or the price with other features included:

✔ **Was kostet das Zimmer pro Nacht?** *(vâs kôs-tet dâs tsî-mer proh nâHt)* (What does the room cost per night?)

✔ **Was kostet eine Übernachtung mit Frühstück?**
(vâs kôs-tet ay-ne uu-bêr-nâH-tûngk mît fruu-shtuuk) (What does accommodation including breakfast cost?)

✔ **Was kostet ein Zimmer mit Vollpension?** *(vâs kôs-tet ayn tsî-mer mît fôl-pâng-zîohn)* (What does a room with full board cost?)

✔ **Was kostet ein Zimmer mit Halbpension?** *(vâs kôs-tet ayn tsî-mer mît hâlp-pâng-zîohn)* (What does a room with half board cost?)

If the room is available and you're happy with the price, you can seal the deal by saying

Können Sie das Zimmer bitte reservieren?
(kuo-nen zee dâs tsî-mer bî-te re-zêr-vee-ren)
(Could you please reserve that room?)

Checking In: Names, Addresses, and Room Numbers

After you arrive at your hotel, you have to check in at the **Rezeption** *(dee rê-tsêp-tsjohn)* (the reception desk). To let the receptionist know that you have made reservations, you say

Ich habe ein Zimmer reserviert. *(îH hah-be ayn tsî-mer rê-zêr-veert)* (I have reserved a room.)

Of course, you also have to let the receptionist know what your name is:

Mein Name ist . . . *(myn nah-me îst . . .)*
(My name is . . .)

How long are you staying?

If you haven't made a reservation, or the receptionist wants to double-check the length of your stay, you may hear the question:

Wie lange bleiben Sie? *(vee lân-ge bly-ben zee)*
(How long are you going to stay?)

To the question about how long you want to stay, you
can reply with the phrase

Ich bleibe / Wir bleiben . . . *(îH bly-be . . . / veer
bly-ben . . .)* (I'm going to stay . . . / We are going
to stay . . .)

Then end the phrase with any of the appropriate
lengths of time:

- ✔ **. . . nur eine Nacht.** *(. . . noor ay-ne nâHt)*
  (. . . just one night.)
- ✔ **. . . drei Tage.** *(. . . dry tah-ge)* (. . . three days.)
- ✔ **. . . eine Woche.** *(. . . ay-ne vô-He)* (. . . one
  week.)

Filling out the registration form

At some hotels, you may have to fill in a form, **das
Formular** *(dâs fôr-mû-lahr)*, at the reception desk as
part of the registration process. The receptionist will
hand you the form, saying something like the following:

Bitte füllen Sie dieses Formular aus. *(bî-te fuu-ln
zee dee-zês fôr-mû-lahr ows)* (Please fill in this
form.)

You may be asked for any of the following information
(often in this order):

- ✔ **Name / Vorname** *(nah-me / fohr-nah-me)*
  (Surname / First Name)
- ✔ **Straße / Nummer (Nr.)** *(shtrah-se / nû-mer)*
  (Street / Number)
- ✔ **Postleitzahl / Wohnort** *(pôst-lyt-tsahl / vohn-ôrt)*
  (zip code / City)
- ✔ **Geburtsdatum / Geburtsort** *(gê-bûrts-dah-tûm /
  gê-bûrts-ôrt)* (Birth date / Place of birth)
- ✔ **Nationalität** *(nâ-tsjoh-nah-lî-tait)* (Nationality)

- **Beruf** *(bê-roof)* (Occupation)
- **Passnummer** *(pâss-nû-mer)* (Passport number)
- **Kraftfahrzeugkennzeichen** *(krâft-fahr-tsoygk-kên-tsy-Hen)* (License plate number)
- **Ort / Datum** *(ôrt / dah-tûm)* (Place / Date)
- **Unterschrift** *(ûn-ter-shrîft)* (Signature)

Understanding the key game

After you've checked in, the receptionist lets you know what your room number is

> **Sie haben Zimmer Nummer 203.** *(zee hah-bn tsî-mer nû-mer tsvy-hûn-dêrt-dry)* (You have room number 203.)

Your room number is usually conveniently written on the key, just as it is in most American hotels.

In some hotels, usually in smaller towns, you may have to leave your key at the reception desk instead of taking it with you when you're going out. When you arrive back at the hotel, you can use either of the following phrases to request your key:

- **Können Sie mir bitte den Schlüssel für Zimmer Nummer. . . geben?** *(kuon-nen zee meer bî-te dehn shluu-sêl fuur tsî-mer nû-mer . . . geh-ben)* (Could you please give me the key for room number . . .?)
- **Den Schlüssel für Zimmer . . . bitte.** *(dehn shluu-sêl fuur tsî-mer . . . bî-te)* (The key for room number . . . please.)

Asking about amenities and facilities

You may also want to find out what kind of services and facilities the hotel offers. For example, does your room have a phone or a minibar? Does the hotel have laundry service?

Your room

When you want to ask about specific features of your room, start with the phrase

Hat das Zimmer . . .? *(hât dâs tsî-mer . . .)* (Does the room have . . .?)

Then end the phrase with any of the following items:

✔ **. . . Kabelfernsehen?** *(. . . kah-bel-fêrn-zehn)* (. . . cable TV?)

✔ **. . . eine Minibar?** *(. . . ay-ne mî-nî-bahr)* (. . . a minibar?)

✔ **. . . Satellitenfernsehen** *(. . . zâtê-lee-ten-fêrn-zehn)* (. . . satellite TV?)

✔ **. . . ein Telefon?** *(. . . ayn tê-le-fohn)* (. . . a phone?)

The hotel

The hotel may offer a number of services. Usually these services are outlined in a pamphlet or menu that you find in your room. However, if you don't find any written clues about services waiting for you in your room, you can call up the reception desk and ask:

Hat das Hotel . . .? *(hât dâs hoh-têl . . .)* (Does the hotel have . . .?)

You can then ask about any of the following services by ending the preceding phrase with:

✔ **. . . einen Faxdienst?** *(. . . ay-nen fâks-deenst)* (. . . a fax machine?)

✔ **. . . eine Hotelgarage?** *(. . . ay-ne hoh-têl-gâ-rah-ge)* (. . . hotel garage?)

✔ **. . . eine Klimaanlage?** *(. . . ay-ne klee-mah-ân-lah-ge)* (. . . air conditioning?)

✔ **. . . einen Parkplatz?** *(. . . ay-nen pârk-plâts)* (. . . parking lot?)

✔ **. . . eine Sauna?** *(. . . ay-ne zow-nah)* (. . . a sauna?)

✔ **. . . ein Schwimmbad?** *(. . . ayn shvîm-baht)*
(. . . a swimming pool?)

✔ **. . . einen Wäschedienst?** *(. . . ay-nen vai-she-deenst)* (. . . laundry service?)

And here are the questions that allow you to inquire about breakfast and room service:

✔ **Wann wird das Frühstück serviert?** *(vân vîrt dâs fruu-shtuuk zêr-veert)* (At what time is breakfast served?)

✔ **Gibt es Zimmerservice?** *(gîpt ês tsî-mer-ser-vîs)* (Is there room service?)

An important part of making your life easier while staying at a hotel is to be able to check if you received any calls. The question to ask is

Hat jemand eine Nachricht für mich hinterlassen? *(hât yeh-mânt ay-ne nahH-rîHt fuur mîH hîn-ter-lâsn)* (Did somebody leave a message for me?)

Words to Know

ausfüllen	ows-fuu-ln	to fill out
Bitte nicht stören!	bî-te nîHt shtuo-rên	Please don't disturb!
bleiben	bly-ben	to stay
das Formular	dâs fôr-mû-lahr	form
der Parkplatz	dehr pârk-plâts	parking lot
der Schlüssel	dehr shluu-sêl	key
der Zimmerservice	dehr tsî-mer-ser-vîs	room service

Checking Out and Paying the Bill

After your stay is over, you have to make arrangements for checking out and paying your bill.

The German language has no exact equivalent for the convenient English term "to check out." The German term you use for checking out of your room is **das Zimmer räumen** *(dâs tsî-mêr roy-men),* which literally translates into "to clear out the room." If you want to inquire at what time you have to leave your room, you ask the following:

>**Bis wann müssen wir das Zimmer räumen?** *(bîs vân muusn veer dâs tsî-mêr roy-men)* (At what time do we have to check out of our room?)

Asking for your bill

To get the reception desk busy preparing your bill, you can say

>**Kann ich bitte die Rechnung haben?** *(kân îH bî-te dee rêH-nûngk hah-bn)* (Can I please get the bill?)

Parting shots at the hotel

If you have to check out of the hotel before you actually want to continue your travels, you may want to leave your luggage for a couple of hours (most hotels will allow you to do this):

>**Können wir unser / Kann ich mein Gepäck bis . . . Uhr hier lassen?** *(kuo-nen veer ûn-zer / kân îH myn ge-pêk bîs . . . oor heer lâssn)* (Can we leave our / Can I leave my luggage here until . . . o'clock?)

As soon as you return to pick up your luggage, you can say

**Können wir / Kann ich bitte unser / mein
Gepäck haben?** *(kuo-nen veer / kân îH bî-te
ûn-zer / myn ge-pêk hah-ben)* (Can we / Can I get
our / my luggage, please?)

Ready to go to the airport or train station? If you want
the receptionist to call you a cab, you ask

Können Sie mir bitte ein Taxi bestellen? *(kuon-
nen zee meer bî-te ayn tâk-see be-shtêl-len)* (Can
you call a cab for me?)

Words to Know

abreisen	âp-ry-zên	to leave
das Gepäck	dâs ge-pêk	luggage
Gute Reise!	gû-te ry-ze	Have a good trip!
selbstverständlich	zêlpst-fêr-shtaint-lîH	Of course

Chapter 11

Dealing with Emergencies

● ●

In This Chapter

▶ Asking for help

▶ Going to the doctor or hospital

▶ Talking to the police

● ●

I hope you'll never need to use the vocabulary and information in this chapter, but it's still a must for any language learner. This chapter assists you in dealing with all kinds of emergency situations, from going to the doctor to reporting a theft.

Asking for Help with Accidents

Memorizing the phrases in this section can help you keep your cool while handling emergencies.

Shouting for help

The following expressions come in handy if you need to call for help:

✔ **Feuer!** *(foy-êr)* (Fire!)

✔ **Holen Sie einen Arzt!** *(hoh-ln zee ay-nen ârtst)* (Get a doctor!)

✔ **Hilfe!** *(hîl-fe)* (Help!)

✔ **Rufen Sie die Polizei!** *(roo-fn zee dee pô-lî-tsy)* (Call the police!)

✔ **Rufen Sie einen Krankenwagen!** *(roo-fn zee ay-nen krânkn-vahgn)* (Call an ambulance!)

✔ **Rufen Sie die Feuerwehr!** *(roo-fn zee dee foy-er-vehr)* (Call the fire department!)

Reporting a problem

If you need to report an accident or have to let people know that you or other people are hurt, this basic vocabulary can help:

✔ **Ich möchte einen Unfall melden.** *(îH muoH-te ay-nen ûn-fâl mêldn)* (I want to report an accident.)

✔ **Ich möchte einen Unfall auf der Autobahn melden.** *(îH muoH-te ay-nen ûn-fâl owf dehr ow-tô-bahn mêldn)* (I want to report an accident on the freeway.)

✔ **Ich bin verletzt.** *(îH bîn fêr-lêtst)* (I am hurt.)

✔ **Es gibt Verletzte.** *(ês gîpt fêr-lêts-te)* (There are injured people.)

Accidents aside, you need to be prepared for other emergencies, such as robbery or theft:

✔ **Ich möchte einen Diebstahl / Raubüberfall melden.** *(îH muoH-te ay-nen deep-shtahl / rowp-uu-bêr-fâl mêldn)* (I want to report a theft / robbery.)

✔ **Haltet den Dieb!** *(hâl-tet dehn deep)* (Catch the thief!)

Asking for English-speaking help

If you find that you can't get the help that you need by speaking German, this is what you say to find out if there's somebody around who speaks English:

Spricht hier jemand Englisch? *(shprîHt heer yeh-mânt êng-lîsh)* (Does anybody here speak English?)

Words to Know

Feuer!	<u>foy</u>-êr	Fire!
Hilfe!	<u>hîl</u>-fe	Help!
Rufen Sie die Polizei!	<u>roo</u>-fn zee dee pô-lî-<u>tsy</u>	Call the police!

Going to the Doctor or Hospital

If you're sick or hurt and need to go to a doctor or to the hospital while you're in a German-speaking country, you need to know the following words:

- ✔ **der Arzt / die Ärztin** *(dehr ârtst / dee <u>êrts</u>-tîn)* (doctor)
- ✔ **die Arztpraxis** *(dee <u>ârtst</u>-prâ-xîs)* (doctor's office)
- ✔ **der Doktor** *(dehr <u>dôk</u>-tohr)* (doctor)
- ✔ **das Krankenhaus** *(dâs <u>krânkn</u>-hows)* (hospital)
- ✔ **die Krankenschwester** *(<u>krâng</u>-kên-shvês-têr)* (female nurse)
- ✔ **die Notaufnahme** *(dee <u>noht</u>-owf-nah-me)* (emergency room)
- ✔ **der Pfleger** *(<u>pfleh</u>-gêr)* (male nurse)

If you're in need of medical help, use these sentences:

- ✔ **Ich brauche einen Arzt.** *(îH <u>brow</u>-He <u>ay</u>-nen ârtst)* (I need a doctor.)

✔ **Wo ist die nächste Arztpraxis / das nächste Krankenhaus?** *(voh îst dee naiH-ste ârtst-prâ-xîs / dâs naiH-ste krânkn-hows)* (Where is the nearest doctor's office / the nearest hospital?)

Describing what ails you

Stomach aching? Feeling feverish? Shooting pains up your neck? Consumed by nausea? Use the following phrases if you want to express that you aren't feeling well and where it hurts:

✔ **Ich fühle mich nicht wohl.** *(îH fuu-le mîH nîHt vohl)* (I'm not feeling well.)

✔ **Ich bin krank.** *(îH bîn krânk)* (I am sick.)

✔ **Ich habe Fieber.** *(îH hah-be fee-ber)* (I have a fever.)

✔ **Mir tut der Hals / Bauch / Rücken weh.** *(meer tût dehr hâlts / bowh / ruu-kn veh)* (My neck / stomach / back hurts.)

✔ **Ich habe Schmerzen im Arm / Bauch.** *(îH hah-be shmêr-tsn îm ârm / bowH)* (I feel pain in the arm / stomach.)

✔ **Ich habe (starke) Bauchschmerzen / Kopf-schmerzen / Zahnschmerzen.** *(îH hah-be shtâr-ke bowH-shmêr-tsn / kôpf-shmêr-tsn / tsahn-shmêr-tsn)* (I have [a severe] stomachache / headache / toothache.)

✔ **Ich habe Halsschmerzen / Rückenschmerzen.** *(îH hah-be hâlts-shmêr-tsn / ruu-kn-shmêr-tsn)* (I have a sore throat / back pain.)

Announcing any special conditions

An important part of getting treatment is to let the doctor know if you're allergic to something or if you have any medical conditions. To do so, start out by saying

Ich bin . . . *(îh bîn . . .)* (I am . . .)

Then finish the sentence with any of the following:

- ✔ **allergisch gegen . . .** *(â-lêr-gîsh geh-gn . . .)* (allergic to . . .)
- ✔ **behindert** *(bê-hîn-dêrt)* (handicapped)
- ✔ **Diabetiker** *(dîa-beh-tî-ker)* (a diabetic)
- ✔ **Epileptiker** *(eh-pî-lêp-tî-ker)* (an epileptic)
- ✔ **schwanger** *(shvâng-er)* (pregnant)

A few specific conditions may require that you begin with:

> **Ich habe . . .** *(îH hah-be . . .)* (I have . . .)

You can end this phrase with any of the following:

- ✔ **ein Herzleiden** *(ayn hêrts-ly-dn)* (a heart condition)
- ✔ **zu hohen / niedrigen Blutdruck** *(tsû hoh-en / nee-drî-gen bloot-drûk)* (high / low blood pressure)

Getting an examination

While you're sitting in the examination room, you may hear some of these questions:

- ✔ **Was haben Sie für Beschwerden?** *(vâs hah-bn zee fuur be-shvehr-dn)* (What complaints do you have?)
- ✔ **Haben Sie Schmerzen?** *(hah-bn zee shmêr-tsn)* (Are you in pain?)
- ✔ **Wo tut es weh?** *(voh toot ês veh)* (Where does it hurt?)
- ✔ **Tut es hier weh?** *(toot ês heer veh)* (Does it hurt here?)
- ✔ **Wie lange fühlen Sie sich schon so?** *(vee lân-ge fuu-len zee zîH shohn zoh)* (How long have you been feeling this way?)

✔ **Sind Sie gegen irgendetwas allergisch?** *(zînt zee geh-gen îr-gênt-êt-vâs ah-lêr-gîsh)* (Are you allergic to something?)

Your doctor may give you one of these instructions:

✔ **Bitte streifen Sie den Ärmel hoch.** *(bî-te shtry-fn zee dehn êr-mel hoH)* (Please pull up your sleeve.)

✔ **Bitte machen Sie den Oberkörper frei.** *(bî-te mâ-Hen zee dehn oh-bêr-kuor-per fry)* (Please take off your shirt.)

✔ **Bitte legen Sie sich hin.** *(bî-te leh-gn zee zîH hîn)* (Please lie down.)

✔ **Machen Sie bitte den Mund auf.** *(mâ-Hn zee bî-te dehn mûnt owf)* (Please open your mouth.)

✔ **Atmen Sie bitte tief durch.** *(aht-men zee bî-te teef dûrH)* (Please take a deep breath.)

✔ **Husten Sie bitte.** *(hoos-tn zee bî-te)* (Please cough.)

Specifying parts of the body

To the question **Wo tut es weh?** *(voh toot ês veh)* (Where does it hurt?), you can answer any of the following:

✔ **der Arm** *(dehr ârm)* (arm)

✔ **das Auge** *(dâs ow-ge)* (eye)

✔ **der Bauch** *(dehr bowH)* (stomach)

✔ **das Bein** *(dâs byn)* (leg)

✔ **die Brust** *(dee brûst)* (chest)

✔ **der Daumen** *(dehr dow-men)* (thumb)

✔ **der Finger** *(dehr fîng-er)* (finger)

✔ **der Fuß** *(dehr foos)* (foot)

✔ **der Fußknöchel** *(dehr foos-knuoHl)* (ankle)

✔ **das Gesicht** *(dâs ge-zîHt)* (face)

✔ **das Haar** *(dâs hahr)* (hair)

✔ **der Hals** *(dehr hâlts)* (neck)

✔ **die Hand** *(dee hânt)* (hand)

✔ **das Herz** *(dâs hêrts)* (heart)

✔ **der Kiefer** *(dehr kee-fr)* (jaw)

✔ **das Knie** *(dâs knee)* (knee)

✔ **der Kopf** *(dehr kôpf)* (head)

✔ **der Magen** *(dehr mah-gn)* (stomach)

✔ **die Lippe** *(dee lî-pe)* (lip)

✔ **der Mund** *(dehr mûnt)* (mouth)

✔ **der Muskel** *(dehr mûs-kl)* (muscle)

✔ **die Nase** *(dee nah-ze)* (nose)

✔ **das Ohr** *(dâs ohr)* (ear)

✔ **der Rücken** *(dehr ruu-kn)* (back)

✔ **die Schulter** *(dee shûl-tr)* (shoulder)

✔ **der Zeh** *(dehr tseh)* (toe)

✔ **die Zunge** *(dee tsûn-ge)* (tongue)

Getting the diagnosis

Now you need to understand what the doctor thinks might be wrong with you. Acquaint yourself with some of these very useful phrases so that you aren't left in the dark:

✔ **Blinddarmentzündung / Lungenentzündung / Mandelentzündung** *(blînt-dârm-ênt-tsuun-dûng / lûngn-ênt-tsuun-dûng / mân-del-ênt-tsuun-dûng)* (appendicitis / pneumonia / tonsillitis)

✔ **die Diagnose** *(dee dî-âg-noh-ze)* (diagnosis)

✔ **eine Entzündung** *(ay-ne ênt-tsuun-dûng)* (an inflammation)

✔ **eine Erkältung** *(ay-ne êr-kêl-tûng)* (a cold)

✔ **eine Grippe** *(ay-ne grî-pe)* (the flu)

✔ **Sie haben . . .** *(zee hah-bn . . .)* (You have . . .)

✔ **Wir müssen eine Röntgenaufnahme machen.**
(veer <u>muu</u>-sn <u>ay</u>-ne <u>ruont</u>-gên-owf-nah-me <u>mâ</u>-Hn)
(We have to take an X-ray.)

✔ **Sie müssen geröntgt werden.** *(zee <u>muu</u>-sn ge-<u>ruonHt</u> <u>vêr</u>-dn)* (You have to get an X-ray.)

✔ **Ihr Knöchel ist gebrochen / verstaucht / ver-renkt.** *(eer <u>knuo</u>-Hêl îst ge-<u>brôHn</u> / fêr-<u>shtowHt</u> / fêr-<u>rênkt</u>)* (Your ankle is broken / sprained / dislocated.)

✔ **Bleiben Sie die nächsten Tage im Bett!** *(<u>bly</u>-bn zee dee <u>naiH</u>-stn <u>tah</u>-ge îm bêt)* (Stay in bed for the next few days.)

Words to Know

Ich bin krank.	îH bîn krânk	I am sick.
Ich brauche einen Arzt.	îH <u>brow</u>-He <u>ay</u>-nen ârtst	I need a doctor.
Wo tut es weh?	voh toot ês veh	Where does it hurt?
Haben Sie Schmerzen?	<u>hah</u>-bn zee <u>shmêr</u>-tsn	Are you in pain?

Getting treatment

After the doctor tells you what the problem is, he or she will advise you what to do. The doctor may ask you one final question before deciding on what treatment is best for you:

Nehmen Sie noch andere Medikamente? *(<u>neh</u>-mn zee nôH <u>ân</u>-de-re meh-dee-kâ-<u>mên</u>-te)* (Are you taking any other medication?)

The doctor may prescribe the following:

✔ **Ich gebe Ihnen . . . / Ich verschreibe Ihnen . . .**
  (îH geh-be ee-nen . . . / îH fêr-shry-be ee-nen . . .)
  (I'll give you . . . / I'll prescribe for you . . .)

✔ **Antibiotika** *(ân-tee-byoh-tî-kâ)* (antibiotics)

✔ **das Medikament / die Medikamente** (pl) *(dâs meh-dee-kâ-mênt / dee meh-dee-kâ-mên-te)* (medication)

✔ **ein Schmerzmittel** *(ayn shmêrts-mîtl)* (a painkiller)

✔ **Tabletten** *(tâ-blêtn)* (pills)

The doctor gives you a prescription, **das Rezept** *(dâs rê-tsêpt),* that you take to a pharmacy, called **die Apotheke** *(dee âpô-teh-ke),* to be filled. The following vocabulary words can help you to understand how to take your medication:

✔ **Bitte, nehmen Sie . . . Tabletten / Teelöffel . . .**
  (bî-te neh-men zee . . . tah-blêtn / teh-luofl . . .)
  (Please take . . . pills / teaspoons . . .)

✔ **dreimal am Tag / täglich** *(dry-mahl âm tahgk / taig-lîH)* (three times a day / daily)

✔ **alle . . . Stunden** *(â-le . . . shtûn-dn)* (every . . . hours)

✔ **vor / nach dem Essen** *(fohr / naH dehm êssn)* (before / after meals)

Finally, the doctor may wish to see you again, saying:

✔ **Kommen Sie in . . . Tagen / einer Woche wieder.** *(kô-mn zee în . . . tah-gn / ay-ner vô-He vee-der)* (Come back in . . . days / one week.)

✔ **Gute Besserung!** *(goo-te bê-se-rûng)* (Feel better!)

Talking to the Police

If you find yourself in the unfortunate place of having to report a robbery to police, use these important expressions:

✔ **Wo ist die nächste Polizeiwache?** *(voh îsst dee naiH-ste pô-lî-tsy-vâ-he)* (Where is the closest police station?)

✔ **Ich möchte einen Diebstahl melden.** *(îH muoH-te ay-nen deep-shtahl mêl-dn)* (I would like to report a theft.)

Describing what was stolen

To describe a theft, you start out by saying

Man hat mir . . . gestohlen. *(mân hât meer . . . ge-shtoh-len)* (Someone has stolen . . .)

You can then finish the sentence by inserting any of the following:

✔ **mein Auto** *(myn ow-toh)* (my car)

✔ **meine Brieftasche / mein Portemonnaie** *(my-ne breef-tâ-she / myn pôr-te-moh-neh)* (my wallet)

✔ **mein Geld** *(myn gêlt)* (my money)

✔ **meinen Pass** *(my-nen pâs)* (my passport)

✔ **meine Tasche** *(my-ne tâ-she)* (my bag)

If you want to express that someone has broken into your house or office, you use the verb **einbrechen** *(ayn-brê-Hen)* (break into):

Man hat bei mir eingebrochen. *(mân hât by meer ayn-ge-brôHn)* (Someone has broken into my room.)

If you're talking about your car, however, you use a similar but slightly different verb, **aufbrechen** *(owf-brê-Hen),* which literally means "to break open":

Man hat mein Auto aufgebrochen. *(mân hât myn ow-tô owf-ge-brôHn)* (Someone has broken into my car.)

The indefinite pronoun **man** *(mân)*, which means one, that is, people in general, comes in handy — and it never changes its ending! For example:

✔ **Man hat seine Tasche gestohlen.** *(mân hât zy-ne tâ-she ge-shtoh-len)* (Someone has stolen his bag.)

✔ **Man hat ihre Tasche gestohlen.** *(mân hât ee-re tâ-she ge-shtoh-len)* (Someone has stolen her bag.)

Answering questions from the police

Being able to describe people is an important language skill, especially if you're talking to the police. In a crime situation, the police may ask you

> **Können Sie die Person beschreiben?** *(kuo-nen zee dee pêr-zohn be-shrybn)* (Can you describe that person?)

Your answer to this question can begin with

> **Die Person hatte . . .** *(dee per-zohn hâ-te . . .)* (The person had . . .)

Then finish the sentence with any of the following: (You can combine traits by saying "und" between any of the following answers.)

✔ **einen Bart / keinen Bart** *(ay-nen bahrt / ky-nen bahrt)* (a beard / no beard)

✔ **blonde / schwarze / rote / graue Haare** *(blôn-de / shvâr-tse / roh-te / grâû-e hah-re)* (blond / black / red / gray hair)

✔ **eine Brille** *(ay-ne brî-le)* (glasses)

✔ **eine Glatze** *(ay-ne glâ-tse)* (a bald head)

Or your answer can begin with **Die Person war . . .** *(dee pêr-zohn vahr . . .)* (The person was . . .) and end with any of the following:

✔ **groß / klein** *(grohs / klyn)* (tall / short)

✔ **ungefähr . . . Meter . . . groß** *(ūn-ge-fair . . . meh-ter . . . grohs)* (approximately . . . meters tall)

✔ **ungefähr . . . Jahre alt** *(ūn-ge-fair . . . yah-re ålt)* (approximately . . . years old)

The police may also ask you the following questions:

✔ **Wann ist das passiert?** *(vån ĩst dås på-seert)* (When did it happen?)

✔ **Wo waren Sie in dem Moment?** *(voh vah-ren zee ĩn dehm moh-mênt)* (Where were you at that moment?)

Protecting your rights abroad

Had enough for the day? If you're really not up to conversing with the law on your own, here are two very important phrases to know:

✔ **Ich brauche einen Anwalt.** *(ĩH brow-he ay-nen ān-vålt)* (I need a lawyer.)

✔ **Ich möchte das Konsulat anrufen.** *(ĩH muoH-te dås kôn-zoo-laht ān-roofn)* (I would like to call the consulate.)

Chapter 12

Ten Favorite German Expressions

. . . .

After you get tuned into German a little, you may suddenly hear people use these German expressions that seem to just slip out at any given moment. You may even have heard some of them already; now take the time to casually use them yourself.

Alles klar!

(â-les klahr)

The literal translation is: "Everything clear." People use it to signal that they understand when somebody explains something to them or to indicate agreement when someone has gone over the details of a plan. In this context, the expression means "Got it!"

Geht in Ordnung.

(geht în ôrd-nûng)

You use this phrase to indicate that you'll take care of something. It translates into "I'll do it."

Kein Problem.

(kayn proh-<u>blehm</u>)

This phrase translates literally into "no problem." Use it to let somebody know that you'll take care of something. You can also agree to a change in plans with this phrase.

Guten Appetit!

(gootn â-pê-<u>teet</u>)

This phrase literally means "Good appetite!" However, this phrase certainly isn't meant as a comment on anyone's good or bad appetite. You say it to each other when you begin to eat or when you see someone eating, much like the English "Enjoy!" — except that German speakers wish each other "Guten Appetit" much more freely.

Deine Sorgen möchte ich haben!

(<u>dy</u>-ne <u>zôr</u>-gn <u>muoH</u>-te îH <u>hah</u>-bn)

This phrase translates: "I would like to have your worries." People often use it facetiously, when a situation seems terrible to one party, but not half as awful to the other.

Das darf doch wohl nicht wahr sein!

(dâs dârf dôH vohl nîHt vahr zâyn)

This expression translates: "This just can't be true!" and what it implies is rendered with one word in English: "Unbelievable."

Mir reicht's!

(meer ryHt's)

This phrase means "It's enough for me" or, to put it into more idiomatic English, "I've had it" or "I've had enough."

Wie schön!

(vee shuon)

The literal translation of this phrase is "How nice!" It can mean that, but sometimes people use it sarcastically, and then it's a way to vent annoyance or exasperation.

Genau.

(ge-now)

This phrase means "exactly," and German speakers use it to show that they agree with the things someone is saying.

Stimmt's?

(shtĩmts)

This phrase translates as "Isn't it true? or "Don't you agree?" Use it when someone wants your confirmation of something just said. You usually answer it with **Stimmt!** *(stĩmt)* meaning "I agree."

Chapter 13

Ten Phrases That Make You Sound Like a Local

• •

This chapter provides you with some typical German expressions that almost everyone who speaks German knows and uses. These phrases are so very German that you may even pass for a native German speaker when you use them.

Das ist ja toll!

(dâs îst yah tôl)

(This is great!) This is the most common German way to express your excitement about something.

Ruf mich an! / Rufen Sie mich an!

(roof mîH an / roofn zee mîH an)

(Call me! informal / formal) If you want to keep in touch with somebody, use this expression.

Was ist los?

(vâs îst lohs)

(What's happening?) This question is most commonly used in the sense of "What's wrong?"

Keine Ahnung.

(<u>ky</u>-ne <u>ah</u>-nûng)

(No idea.) This phrase is the short version of **Ich habe keine Ahnung**. *(îH <u>hah</u>-be <u>ky</u>-ne <u>ah</u>-nûng)* (I have no idea.) and is frequently used to express that you know nothing about the matter in question.

Gehen wir!

(gehn veer)

(Let's go!) Use this phrase if you want to get going!

Nicht zu fassen!

(nîHt tzoo <u>fâ</u>-sen)

(I can't believe it!) If you want to express disbelief, concern, or agitation, try this typically German phrase.

Du hast Recht! / Sie haben Recht!

(doo hâst rêHt / zee <u>hah</u>-bn rêHt)

(You're right! informal / formal) This phrase is the most typical way of expressing agreement in German.

Auf keinen Fall!

(owf ky-nen fâl)

(No way!) Literally, this expression means "In no case!" and you want to use it if you want to make your disagreement very clear.

Nicht schlecht!

(nîHt shlêHt)

(Not bad!) As in English, this phrase not only means that something isn't too bad — it's also a reserved way of expressing appreciation and approval.

Das ist mir (völlig) egal.

(dâs îst meer [vuo-lîg] ê-gahl)

(I don't mind. / I don't care.) You can use this phrase to express that you don't mind if it's one way or another, or that you couldn't care less.

Index

Notes

Notes

FOR DUMMIES

The easy way to get more done and have more fun